MATH
By All Means®

GEOMETRY
Grades 1–2

by Chris Confer

A MARILYN BURNS REPLACEMENT UNIT

MATH SOLUTIONS PUBLICATIONS

Math Solutions Publications
A division of
Marilyn Burns Education Associates
150 Gate 5 Road, Suite 101
Sausalito, CA 94965
www.mathsolutions.com

Copyright ©1994 by Math Solutions Publications
Reprinted October 2005

ISBN-10: 0-941355-08-X
ISBN-13: 978-0-941355-08-7

Editorial Direction: Lorri Ungaretti
Art direction and design: Aileen Friedman
Typesetting: Rad H. M. Proctor
Page makeup: Aileen Friedman and David Healy, First Image
Illustrations: David Healy, First Image
Cover background and border designs: Barbara Gelfand

This book is printed on recycled paper in the United States of America.

A Message from Marilyn Burns

We at Math Solutions Professional Development believe that teaching math well calls for increasing our understanding of the math we teach, seeking deeper insights into how children learn mathematics, and refining our lessons to best promote students' learning.

Math Solutions Publications shares classroom-tested lessons and teaching expertise from our faculty of Math Solutions Inservice instructors as well as from other respected math educators. Our publications are part of the nationwide effort we've made since 1984 that now includes

- more than five hundred face-to-face inservice programs each year for teachers and administrators in districts across the country;
- annually publishing professional development books, now totaling more than fifty titles and spanning the teaching of all math topics in kindergarten through grade 8;
- four series of videotapes for teachers, plus a videotape for parents, that show math lessons taught in actual classrooms;
- on-site visits to schools to help refine teaching strategies and assess student learning; and
- free online support, including grade-level lessons, book reviews, inservice information, and district feedback, all in our quarterly *Math Solutions Online Newsletter*.

For information about all of the products and services we have available, please visit our Web site at *www.mathsolutions.com*. You can also contact us to discuss math professional development needs by calling (800) 868-9092 or by sending an e-mail to *info@mathsolutions.com*.

We're always eager for your feedback and interested in learning about your particular needs. We look forward to hearing from you.

A DIVISION OF MARILYN BURNS EDUCATION ASSOCIATES

PREFACE

This unit was originally developed when Bonnie Tank and I launched The Grade 2 Mathematics Project in the 1990–1991 school year. In this project we developed second grade units that were used by teachers in the San Francisco Bay Area and in the Tucson Unified School District Chapter 1 Mathematics Project. As an Instructional Support Teacher for the Tucson project, Chris Confer had the chance to try the units with teachers and children, so she had several years of experience teaching the units before beginning to write. She has brought to this geometry unit what I hope all teachers will bring to instructional materials—an individual perspective on the activities and how to use them with students.

Chris and I spent many months communicating back and forth about various aspects of the unit. We considered large issues: How should we handle the assessment of children's geometric understanding? What help can we offer teachers whose students have difficulty writing? Should a particular activity be a whole class lesson, a menu activity, or even be included at all? We talked about smaller issues: What's the best size for the square used in an activity? Is a particular pedagogical note appropriate and helpful in this particular section? What are the implications of a certain word or phrase? Because I had taught the unit to second graders the previous year, we were able to compare our teaching experiences. Sometimes, after one of our discussions, Chris returned to the classroom and tried something different with her students.

In reflecting on the process of working with Chris on this book, I realize how my own thinking was stretched by Chris's perspectives. I do much of my classroom teaching in isolation, without the opportunity to collaborate or share experiences with colleagues. Becoming engrossed in Chris's manuscript and talking through issues with her gave me a way to reflect on my own teaching. This collaboration will serve me the next time I teach the unit to children or present it to teachers.

Chris helped me broaden my view of classroom assessment through her "Linking Assessment with Instruction" sections in the whole class lessons. In these sections, Chris provides a fresh look at assessing children and reminds us of the importance of examining children's attitudes and approaches to learning along with their conceptual understanding. She also gives concrete guidelines for thinking about incorporating this aspect of assessment into classroom practice.

What I've come to learn about writing is that additional revision is always possible and that you can tinker and refine manuscripts indefinitely. Chris and I finally agreed to let go of the manuscript and send it on its way to become a book. After the unit was typeset, I reread it. I was pleased. More than pleased, I'm thrilled. I'm still excited by the unit, motivated by the activities, and fascinated by Chris's descriptions of the responses from her students.

I hope that the book offers teachers substantive help for providing children rich and engaging experiences with geometric ideas. We welcome your feedback.

All of the "From the Classroom" vignettes describe what happened when the unit was taught in a second-grade class. However, the grade level span assigned to the unit indicates that it is suitable for grades one and two. We've made this grade-level designation for two reasons. We know that in any class, there is typically a span in students' interests and abilities, and the activities in the unit have been designed to respond to such a span. Also, teachers who have taught the unit have found it successful with children in several grade levels and have reported that the activities are accessible and appropriate to a range of students.

Marilyn Burns
January 1994

Acknowledgments

Special thanks for the insight and support provided by the students, staff, and administrators with whom this unit was developed and tested.

Chapter 1/Exxon Mathematics and Science Project, Tucson Unified School District, Arizona

Ochoa Elementary School, Chapter 1, Tucson Unified School District, Arizona

Drachman Primary Magnet School, Chapter 1, Tucson Unified School District, Arizona

Davis Bilingual Learning Center, Exxon Grant, Tucson Unified School District, Arizona

This book is dedicated to my husband, children, and parents.

CONTENTS

INTRODUCTION

A class of second graders sat on the rug, expectantly. "What do you know about geometry?" I asked the children.

"Geometry!" said Danny. "I know what *that* is! It's like when you study rocks or the earth or the United States." Danny had stood up in his enthusiasm; he sat down again, the picture of confidence.

After a moment, I figured out what Danny meant. "Oh," I said, "you're talking about 'geology' or 'geography.' And those words *do* sound a lot like 'geometry.' But they mean different things. Geometry is part of what we study when we learn about mathematics."

I showed the children a large sheet of chart paper on which I had listed the math strands—number, geometry, measurement, probability, statistics, logic, patterns, functions—and pointed out the word "geometry." "When we study geometry," I explained, "we think about shapes, how they're made, and what we can do with them."

The children eagerly looked around the room and began naming shapes that they saw.

"The paper's a rectangle," Javier told us.

"And the ceiling's got squares," Stacy said.

"Here's a triangle," Alejandra added, touching her nose.

"Teacher! Teacher!" the children cried as they pointed around the room and identified more shapes. Steve noticed that the top of the water cooler was a circle. Then Alejandra showed us the rectangular chalkboard. I also heard some confusion in terminology. Alma identified the rectangular table top as a square; Jonathan called the top of a box a triangle.

I wanted to get a sense of the range of the children's understanding, so I posed a question to the class. "What is a triangle?" I asked.

Many children raised their hands. I called on all who wanted the chance to respond. Typically, children explained that triangles had three points or three sides or three corners.

Adrian offered his idea visually. He traced a triangle shape in the air and said, "It looks like this."

"Can you describe in words what a triangle looks like?" I probed.

Adrian shrugged, a bit shy and unsure.

"I can," Francisca volunteered. "There's a point on top," she said, "and it has a straight bottom."

A few children expressed erroneous ideas.

"Triangles are a square," Raul reported.

"Some triangles are round," Elena said.

Children's differing ideas didn't surprise me. I've come to expect a range of awareness and understanding from students, both with properties of shapes and with geometric terminology. Also, in this class, there is variation in the languages children choose to use when expressing ideas. About 25 percent of the children communicate mostly in Spanish, another 25 percent primarily in English, and about half of the children are bilingual.

Goals for Geometry Instruction

Traditionally, instruction in geometry has focused largely on recognition of regular geometric shapes and memorization of their names and basic characteristics. Geometric ideas are often taught apart from real-life contexts and without physical materials, relying on textbook pages to provide instruction. It is not unusual for children to have limited experience with exploring geometric properties and investigating relationships among shapes.

Geometry has not been emphasized in the elementary mathematics curriculum for several reasons. Teachers frequently feel the pressure exerted by standardized tests, which focus on computation. Most parents believe that mathematics is the study of numbers, and this belief often defines their expectations for children. Teachers themselves may have had limited or negative experiences with geometry. For many, their last instruction was in a high school class where geometric ideas were presented abstractly, with a heavy focus on theorems and proofs.

These realities may explain traditional classroom practices, but they do not justify them. A nationwide movement, spearheaded by the National Council of Teachers of Mathematics (NCTM), challenges us to change in a fundamental way the mathematics instruction that we offer our students. The NCTM's *Curriculum and Evaluation Standards for School Mathematics* (1989) highlights the significance of geometry and spatial sense. It states: "Geometry is an important component of the K–4 mathematics curriculum because geometric knowledge, relationships and insights are useful in everyday situations and are connected to other mathematical topics and school subjects. Geometry helps us represent and describe in an orderly manner the world in which we live" (page 48).

The Standards also address how this knowledge can best be developed: "In learning geometry, children need to investigate, experiment, and explore

with everyday objects and other physical materials. Exercises that ask children to visualize, draw, and compare shapes in various positions will help develop their spatial sense" (page 48).

These recommendations signal a shift toward a broader view of geometry instruction. No longer is the focus on memorization of the names of geometric shapes. Instead, children must develop intuition and understanding about the properties of shapes, how shapes relate to one another, and what happens when shapes are combined or divided. Instruction must allow children to construct their own understanding of concepts by exploring the same idea in different contexts. Children must have opportunities to verbalize their theories and ideas, explore them in different contexts, confront their confusions, and refine their theories, moving on to more complete understanding over time.

The experiences children bring with them from home, such as building with blocks and Legos or hammering boats out of wood, have a direct impact on their spatial abilities. Boys traditionally have more of these kinds of experiences than girls, which may explain the better spatial skills they sometimes have.

Spatial skills are critical for many careers, such as engineering, construction, and science. Teachers must provide *all* children with access to careers such as these. Both girls and boys need opportunities to play with blocks and build with various materials. All children, regardless of their capability with numbers, must have chances to construct and manipulate shapes.

What's in the Unit?

This unit on geometry was created to respond to the current recommendations for instruction. In six weeks of instruction, children are given a variety of problem-solving experiences with geometry in real-world contexts. Students develop spatial understanding as they manipulate shapes, fold and cut paper, create and then sort shapes, and design patchwork patterns. Geometry is integrated with other strands of mathematics, including number, logical thinking, patterns, and statistics.

All children are involved in the same activities. The activities are designed to offer a broad spectrum that accommodates children's different spatial abilities and interests. Throughout the unit, children work with concrete materials. They solve problems, explore patterns, work on puzzles, and sort shapes. Children are continually encouraged to rely on their own methods for finding solutions.

The children participate in whole class lessons, work cooperatively in pairs or small groups, and complete individual assignments. Writing is an integral part of students' math learning. Homework is used to further class experiences as well as to communicate with parents about their children's classroom learning.

Children's Responses to the Unit

As I expected, the children I worked with responded differently to the activities in the unit—in the ways they thought about the geometric ideas and demonstrated their understanding.

Danny, for example, once told me that he had built a go-cart with his big brother, so that's why making a rocket out of shapes was easy for him. And he did show a lot of facility with spatial reasoning; he easily described the components of shapes in different ways, and he could rotate and reposition shapes in his mind. Danny often characterized shapes as pictures: the hexagon was a fox to him and the pentagon a rocket.

In class, Danny seemed to thrive on attention. In any group situation he made his many ideas and opinions known, sometimes blocking off other children's attempts to participate. When working individually or with a partner, however, Danny was less motivated. He especially disliked putting his thoughts into writing. Danny would write a sentence or two and then come to me. "Is this enough?" he would ask. I usually expressed interest in his ideas and then asked him to write more details about what he actually did. For example, after several such encounters during the *Square Designs* menu activity, Danny wrote: *When I did this I forphmed these tingols* [triangles] *It was very ezzey. I foldit 3 time and I kate it and I got this shape.*

Elena was fascinated by shapes. She spent long periods of time putting shapes together and seeing what new shapes she could make. Elena's ability to visualize was exceptional; at a glance she could predict how to reposition a set of shapes to make a certain design.

Although Elena communicated her ideas easily by speaking, she was frustrated by writing. At the beginning of the unit, she refused to write. Elena was a beginning reader, and she did not have the confidence to use what she knew about letter sounds to put her ideas in writing. I approached her in two ways. On days when she seemed overwhelmed or frustrated, I had her dictate her ideas and I wrote them down. Other times I encouraged Elena to try to write on her own. Over time, she learned to use strategies such as completing prompts that I offered the class, spelling words the way they sounded to her, asking friends for help, or using words displayed in the room. I was pleased when, at the end of the unit, Elena proudly showed me what she had written about triangles: *wen de kate pizza.* And she was able to read it: "When they cut pizza."

Shapes were sometimes a mystery to Martha. She struggled to change a three-sided shape on the geoboard into a four-sided shape. And it didn't occur to her that rotating a triangle would allow it to fit nicely into a space in a puzzle.

But Martha seemed to find the investigations easier as the unit progressed. She enjoyed combining shapes to make patchwork patterns. She wrote about her nine-patch pattern: *I uesd a squares and a triangles and dimonds triangles has for sides and a square has for sides to. I uesd 11 shapes to make a dosane* [design]. *you could call the square and the triangle you cold call them quadrilaterals. from a square to make a triangl you get a square and cat* [cut] *in the mitle. to make a dimond you trned the square. to make a square you get a square.*

I can't assume that Martha's math ability was exclusively the result of this unit. But I do believe the unit gave her the opportunity to explore shapes in ways that made sense to her, to listen to other children's thinking about geometry, and to confront misconceptions in a supportive environment.

The challenge of teaching is to find activities that capture children's imagination, give them access to mathematical ideas, and allow them to construct their own understanding. Not all children respond with the same interest to the same activities or learn equally well from them. Therefore, the unit provides a range of activities to help each child find a way to learn about geometry.

The Structure of This Book

The instructional directions are organized into four components: *Whole Class Lessons, Menu Activities, Assessments,* and *Homework.* In addition, the Children's Books section describes children's books that can be integrated into the unit. Blackline masters needed for the activities, as well as a bibliography, are also included.

Whole Class Lessons

Six whole class lessons, each requiring one or two class periods, introduce students to different ways of investigating shapes. Children have experiences cutting squares and putting the pieces together to make new shapes. They fold squares to create new shapes and learn the names of those shapes. They explore triangles using geoboards and combine Pattern Block triangles to create new shapes. They sort shapes in a variety of ways. They create patchwork patterns. As students are engaged with whole class lessons, they acquire and develop the ability to use standard geometric terminology.

The instructional directions for each lesson are presented in four sections:

Overview gives a brief description of the lesson.

Before the Lesson outlines the preparation needed before teaching the lesson.

Teaching Directions gives step-by-step instructions for presenting the lesson.

From the Classroom describes what happened when the lesson was taught to second graders. The vignette helps bring alive the instructional guidelines by giving an over-the-shoulder look into a classroom, telling how lessons were actually organized, how students reacted, and how the teacher responded. The vignettes are not offered as standards of what "should" happen but as a record of what can happen with children.

Linking Assessment with Instruction provides observation guidelines that relate to the specific content of the lesson and help teachers learn about individual students' spatial abilities and understanding of geometry.

Menu Activities

The menu is a collection of activities that children do independently, either individually or in pairs. The tasks on the menu give children a variety of experiences with geometry but are not hierarchical; they do not conceptually build upon one another. The menu tasks pose problems, set up situations, and ask questions that help children work with geometric relationships. Seven activities are included in the menu. Students work on some activities individually and on others with partners.

The instructional directions for each menu activity are presented in five sections:

Overview gives a brief description of the activity.

Before the Lesson outlines the preparation needed before the activity is introduced.

Getting Started gives instructions for introducing the activity.

From the Classroom describes what happened when the activity was introduced to second graders. As with the Whole Class Lessons, the vignette gives a view into an actual classroom, describing how the teacher gave directions and how the students responded.

For additional information about the menu system, see the introduction to the Menu Activities section that begins on page 77.

Assessments

The unit suggests both informal and formal ways to assess what children understand. The "Linking Assessment with Instruction" section in each whole class lesson provides suggestions for informal assessments in the context of classroom instruction. These suggestions are not meant to be comprehensive but rather to highlight the kinds of student responses that teachers might observe and to offer explanations about how children's responses relate to their mathematical development.

The unit also offers five formal assessments: One is suggested for the beginning of the unit to reveal what the children already know about geometry; the others are recommended for the second half of the unit, after students have had experience with some of the unit activities. These assessments are listed in the Table of Contents and are identified in the unit by gray bars in the margins.

For specific information about assessing understanding, see the introduction to the Assessments section that begins on page 17.

Homework

Homework assignments have two purposes: They extend the work children are doing in class, and they inform parents about the learning experiences their children are having. Six homework assignments are suggested.

Blackline Masters

A blackline master with directions for each menu activity is provided along with additional blackline masters as needed for activities.

Children's Books

Reading appropriate children's books can help extend students' understanding of geometric ideas and help children appreciate geometry in their world. At the same time, it is important to give literature its due by allowing children the opportunity simply to enjoy a story for its own sake before discussing the geometry concepts that it contains. A suggested list of children's books is provided for some whole class lessons.

The following books are an integral part of this unit. These and other books that support geometry concepts are listed and described in the Children's Book section. (See page 153.)

A Cloak for the Dreamer by Aileen Friedman

Eight Hands Round: A Patchwork Alphabet by Ann Whitford Paul

Shapes, Shapes, Shapes by Tana Hoban

Supporting Beginning Writers

This unit's approach to mathematics often requires children to explain their thinking in writing. While some children do so easily, others are beginning writers who need support. Teachers can encourage children to write the letters they think are in the words ("invented spelling"), draw pictures, ask other children for help, or use words that are displayed in the room as resources. Some children might need even more support. Often teachers take dictation from these children, writing down what they say.

Beginning writers frequently come to a stage when they are able to read their own writing but others, including the teacher, cannot. Many teachers ask children to read their writing aloud and then rewrite the confusing parts on a Post-it™ Note, explaining to the child, "I might need this to help me remember." Affixing the Post-it to the child's paper honors the child's best effort by leaving it intact while taking into account the teacher's need to recall the child's words. Other teachers choose to write the clarification at the bottom of the paper or directly above the confusing word.

Notes About Classroom Organization

Setting the Stage for Cooperation

Throughout much of the unit, children are asked to work cooperatively, sometimes in pairs and sometimes in small groups. Interaction is an important ingredient for students' intellectual development. They learn from interaction with one another as well as with adults.

Teachers who have taught the unit report different systems for organizing children for cooperative work. Some put pairs of numbers in a bag and have children draw to choose partners. Some assign partners. Some have seatmates work together. Others let children choose their own partners.

Some teachers have students work with the same partner for the entire unit. Others let children change partners for each activity. When teachers allow choice, they spend a good deal of time talking with children about the importance of learning to work with all children, not just their best friends, and being sensitive to the feelings of others. One teacher reported that she makes the rule that children have to work with a different partner for each menu activity; this rule gives children choice within a structure that encourages them to vary their partner choices. Some teachers don't have children work with specific partners but with the other children who are working on the same activity at that time.

The system for organizing children matters less than the underlying classroom attitude. What's important is that children are encouraged to work together, listen to one another's ideas, and be willing to help classmates. Students should see their classroom as a safe place, where cooperation and collaboration are valued and expected. This does not mean, of course, that children never work individually. However, it does respect the principle that interaction fosters learning and, therefore, that cooperative group work is basic to the culture of the classroom.

A System for the Menu Activities

Teachers report several different ways to organize the menu activities. Some teachers use a copy machine to enlarge the blackline masters of the menu tasks onto 11-by-17-inch paper, mount them on construction paper or tagboard, and post them. Although the teacher introduces each activity to the entire class, individual students can later refer to the posted directions for clarification, then return to their seats to work. (Note: A set of posters with menu activity directions for this unit is available from Cuisenaire Company of America.)

Rather than enlarge and post the tasks, other teachers duplicate about a half dozen of each and make them available for children to take to their seats. Mounting them on tagboard makes the copies more durable. For either of the above alternatives, children take materials from the general supply and return them when they finish their work or at the end of class.

Some teachers prefer to assign different stations in the classroom for the tasks. For each activity, they place a copy of the task and the worksheets and materials needed in a cardboard carton or rubber tub. At the beginning of menu time, monitors distribute the tubs to the stations. The number of children who can work at any station is determined by the number of chairs available.

Each of these systems encourages students to be independent and responsible for their learning. They are allowed to spend the amount of time needed on any one task and make choices about the sequence in which they work on tasks. Children who are interested may even revisit tasks and do them again, perhaps in a different way.

How Children Record

Teachers also use different procedures to organize the way children record. Some prepare folders for each child, either by folding 12-by-18-inch

construction paper in half or by using regular file folders, and require children to record individually even when they work cooperatively. Some teachers prepare folders for partners and have the partners collaborate on their written work. Other teachers don't use folders but have students place their finished work in the teacher's "In" basket.

Some teachers have children indicate on a class list when they have completed an activity. Others have them copy the list of menu activities and check off those they have completed; some duplicate the blackline master on page 166 for this use. It's important that the recording system is clear to the class and helps keep the teacher informed about children's progress.

Managing Materials and Supplies

Teachers who have taught this unit report they gave children time to explore the manipulative materials they needed to use. Most devoted several weeks at the beginning of the year to free exploration of materials. Children may need additional opportunities for free exploration from time to time throughout the year. Watch the children; when they begin surreptitiously to build designs with Pattern Blocks or make pictures with geoboards, they may need more time to explore the materials.

All teachers who have taught this unit gave their students guidelines for the care and storage of materials.

Materials

The following materials are needed for the unit:
- Geoboards with rubber bands, at least one board per pair of children or, if possible, one per child
- Pattern Blocks, one set of 250 blocks for each group of four

General Classroom Supplies

- Scissors, at least one for each pair of children
- Tape
- Glue
- Rulers, one for each group of four
- Ample supplies of paper, including newsprint, chart paper, and construction paper

Blackline Masters

Blackline masters for templates and patterns are needed for specific activities. Most teachers choose to have supplies of each sheet available for children to take when needed.

A Suggested Daily Schedule

Predicting how children will respond as the unit unfolds is not possible. However, it's helpful to think through the entire unit and make an overall teaching plan that you can change and adjust. The following day-to-day schedule is a suggested six-week guide. It offers a plan that varies the pace of daily instruction by interweaving days for teaching whole class lessons, introducing menu activities, giving classroom time for menu work, and leading class discussions about the children's work.

Class discussions of menu activities are included throughout the day-to-day plan. These are typically scheduled several days or more after the menu activity was introduced, giving children time to experience the activity before being asked to participate in a class discussion. Since students will be working on menu activities at their own pace and completing them at different times, it's important to check with children about their progress. At times, you might mention to children that they'll be discussing a particular activity the next day and should be sure to do it so they can contribute to the discussion. Although times for class discussions are suggested in the plan, use your judgment about when it's best to have them. For general information about the importance of class discussions, see the Menu Activities introduction on pages 77–79. For suggestions about how to conduct specific discussions, check the "From the Classroom" section for each menu activity.

Six homework assignments are suggested for the unit. (See Homework section, pages 159–164.) Two of them relate specifically to lessons in the unit and appear in the daily schedule: *Hold and Fold* is a follow-up to the *Hold and Fold* whole class lesson, and *A Class Quilt* extends the *Nine-Patch Patterns* menu activity. Each of the other four homework assignments— *Search for Squares, Search for Rectangles, Search for Triangles,* and *Search for Hexagons*—asks children to look for examples of a specific shape in objects at home. Give these assignments at any time during the unit. Asterisks mark possible days for these four "search for" assignments. Be sure to assign them on days when you can discuss the children's work the following day.

The Children's Book section (see pages 153–157) presents books that relate to the geometric ideas in the unit and are suitable for reading to the class. Three of these books—*Shapes, Shapes, Shapes; A Cloak for the Dreamer;* and *Eight Hands Round*—are used in specific lessons and are included in the daily schedule. However, the schedule does not mention times for reading the other books; choose those you wish to read and when to do so as the unit unfolds.

Day 1   Assessment: What Is a Triangle?

After children have completed the assessment, read *Shapes, Shapes, Shapes.* Then ask the children to look around the room and tell what shapes they notice. *(Possible day for a "Search for" homework assignment.)

Day 2   Whole Class Lesson: Rocket Discovery

Introduce the lesson, then have the children make rockets from cutting paper squares.

Day 3   **Whole Class Lesson: Hold and Fold**

Show children how to fold paper squares and then have them look for shapes they can make. Give the homework assignment *Hold and Fold.*

Day 4   **Introduce Two Menu Activities: Rocket Shapes, Square Designs**

Begin class by inviting children to report their experiences at home doing the homework assignment *Hold and Fold.* Then present the directions for the two menu activities. Students choose one of the activities to work on for the remainder of the class.

Day 5   **Menu**

Students continue work on the menu activities. *(Possible day for a "Search for" homework assignment.)

Day 6   **Whole Class Lesson: A Cloak for the Dreamer**

Read and discuss the book *A Cloak for the Dreamer.* Have students create patchwork designs using one shape.

Day 7   **Introduce Menu Activity: Cloak Patterns**

Begin by having students discuss their work from yesterday's whole class lesson *A Cloak for the Dreamer.* Then present the directions for the menu activity and let students continue work on the menu. Direct children who haven't yet tried the *Rocket Shapes* menu activity to begin with it so that they can participate in tomorrow's class discussion.

Day 8   **Menu**

Begin class by having children discuss their experiences working on *Rocket Shapes.* Then let students choose and work on activities from the menu. *(Possible day for a "Search for" homework assignment.)

Day 9   **Menu**

Begin class by directing children who haven't yet done *Square Designs* on the menu to begin with it so that they can participate in tomorrow's class discussion about the activity. Then let children choose and work on activities from the menu.

Day 10   **Menu**

Begin class by having children discuss their experiences working on *Square Designs.* Then let them choose and work on activities from the menu.

Day 11   **Whole Class Lesson: Triangles on the Geoboard**

Introduce the lesson, then have children make triangles on the geoboard and transfer them to dot paper.

Day 12   **Whole Class Lesson: Triangles on the Geoboard (continued)**

Continue with the lesson, leading a class discussion in which the children sort the triangles in several ways.

Day 13   Introduce Menu Activity: More Shapes on the Geoboard

Begin class by asking children who have finished the menu activity *Cloak Patterns* to show their patterns for the class to discuss. Then present the directions for *More Shapes on the Geoboard* and have students choose and work on activities from the menu. *(Possible day for a "Search for" homework assignment.)

Day 14   Menu

Begin class by directing children who haven't done *More Shapes on the Geoboard* to begin with it so they can participate in tomorrow's class discussion about the activity. Then let students choose and work on activities from the menu.

Day 15   Menu

Begin class by sorting the children's shapes from *More Shapes on the Geoboard*. Then let students choose and work on activities from the menu.

Day 16   Introduce Menu Activity: Nine-Patch Patterns

Begin class by discussing more of the children's patterns from the menu activity *Cloak Patterns*. Then read *Eight Hands Round* to the class and discuss the patterns in the book. Finally, present the directions for the menu activity and have students continue work on the menu.

Day 17   Assessment: Describing Shapes

Have children write about the shapes they made from the menu activity *More Shapes on the Geoboard*. As children finish and you accept their work, have them choose a menu activity. *(Possible day for a "Search for" homework assignment.)

Day 18   Menu

Begin class with a discussion about the menu, asking children to talk about their favorite activities. You may also show student work that models the kind of work you'd like all of them to do. Then have them choose and work on activities from the menu.

Day 19   Whole Class Lesson: Shapes with Pattern Block Triangles

Students explore the different shapes that can be made with two, three, four, and five Pattern Block triangles.

Day 20   Introduce Menu Activity: Shapes with Six Triangles

Present the directions for the menu activity and have students continue work on the menu. Direct children who haven't yet done the menu activity *Nine-Patch Patterns* to begin with it so that they can participate in tomorrow's class discussion about the activity.

Day 21   Assessment: Shapes Inside Shapes

Begin class by discussing the children's nine-patch patterns. Then ask the children to write about the shapes inside their nine-patch patterns. As children finish and you accept their work, let them choose a menu activity.

Day 22   **Introduce Menu Activity: Shapes with Six Squares**

Present the directions for the menu activity and have students continue work on the menu. Give the homework assignment *A Class Quilt.*

Day 23   **Menu**

Begin class by telling the children that tomorrow you'll be discussing their work from *Shapes with Six Triangles.* Collect children's patchwork designs from *A Class Quilt* homework assignment; save for Day 27. Let students choose and work on activities from the menu. *(Possible day for a "Search for" homework assignment.)

Day 24   **Menu**

Begin class by discussing the children's work from *Shapes with Six Triangles.* Collect patchwork designs from *A Class Quilt* homework from children who hadn't yet handed them in. Then let students choose and work on activities from the menu.

Day 25   **Whole Class Lesson: Culminating Activity—**
Quilts from Nine-Patch Patterns (Part 1)

Introduce the activity and have children begin working on their nine-patch patterns.

Day 26   **Whole Class Lesson: Culminating Activity—**
Quilts from Nine-Patch Patterns (Part 2)

Introduce Part 2 of the lesson and let children continue work on their quilt patterns and quilts.

Day 27   **Menu**

Begin class by posting and discussing the children's patchwork designs from *A Class Quilt* homework; arrange the squares into a quilt. Then let children choose and work on activities from the menu.

Day 28   **Assessment: Shape Walk**

Read *Shapes, Shapes, Shapes* again to the class. Then take the children on a neighborhood walk to look for geometric shapes and write about their discoveries.

Day 29   **Menu**

Begin class by directing children who haven't posted shapes from the menu activity *Shapes with Six Squares* to do so for tomorrow's discussion. Then let students choose and work on activities from the menu.

Day 30   **Assessment: What Is a Triangle? (Revisited)**

Begin class by discussing the menu activity *Shapes with Six Squares.* Then have children do the same assessment as they did on the first day of the unit. Students who finish early can choose and work on activities from the menu. (This is the last day of the unit, but leave the chart posted for *Shapes with Six Squares,* so children who are interested can continue the investigation.)

A Letter to Parents

Although parents will learn about their children's experiences from homework assignments and papers sent home, you may want to give them general information about the unit before you begin. The following is a sample letter that informs parents about the goals of the unit and introduces them to some of the activities their children will be doing.

Dear Parent,

Our next math unit will be an exploration of geometry. Studying geometry is important for children, as it helps them connect mathematics to the real world. It also helps them broaden their idea of mathematics beyond the study of numbers.

To build their spatial abilities, children will manipulate, fold, and construct shapes. They will compare shapes and sort them by their various properties. Through these experiences, they will begin to see relationships among geometric figures.

The language of geometry will be used throughout the unit. Your child will begin to understand and use many geometric terms, including *triangle, quadrilateral, square, rectangle, parallelogram, trapezoid, pentagon, hexagon,* and others.

The children will be engaged in a variety of activities to build their understanding of shapes and relationships among them. They will learn how a square can be folded into many different shapes, and they'll bring the square home for you to investigate. They will use geoboards to discover properties of triangles and other shapes. And they will use Pattern Blocks to explore the different shapes that can be made with four, five, and six triangles. They will also try putting different shapes together to make pleasing patterns for patchwork designs.

It's helpful for children to relate their geometry experiences at school to the world around them. That is why, from time to time, the children will be asked to find specific shapes at home. I encourage you to engage in these activities with your child.

Also, the class will be involved in making patchwork designs, and it would be nice for the students to see actual quilts. If you have a quilt that you'd be willing to display in our classroom, please let me know.

I hope you will have a chance to talk to your child about what he or she is learning. Please feel free to visit our classroom any time.

Sincerely,

A Final Comment

The decisions teachers make every day in the classroom are the heart of teaching. This book attempts to provide clear and detailed information about lessons and activities, but it is not a recipe that can be followed step by step. Rather, the unit offers options that require teachers to make decisions in several areas: sequencing activities, organizing the classroom, grouping children, communicating with parents, and dealing with the needs of individual children. Keep in mind that there is no "best" or "right" way to teach the unit. The aim is for children to engage in mathematical investigations, be inspired to think and reason, and enjoy their learning.

CONTENTS

ASSESSMENTS

Assessing children's understanding is an ongoing process of collecting information about students' mathematical knowledge, interests, and aptitudes. In the area of geometry, many second graders are familiar with the names of basic geometric shapes—square, circle, triangle, and rectangle. They may have learned these words from hearing them at home or from earlier school experiences. Most children, however, do not fully understand the properties of these shapes and how the shapes relate to one another. They might not have thought about how the shapes are used in our world and how they can be combined with other shapes for new purposes.

Geometry assessment customarily revolves around having children identify and name basic shapes. The questions often emphasize terminology rather than understanding. Assessment in this unit has a different goal: to help teachers assess students' spatial abilities and understanding of geometric relationships. This unit suggests two general approaches to assessment. One is to make assessment an integral part of classroom instruction and the second is to give special assignments for the purpose of assessing students' understanding.

Linking Assessment with Instruction

One way to collect information about what students understand is to do so informally during the regular course of classroom instruction, both in whole class discussions and when students are working individually or in pairs on menu activities and other assignments. Examples of informal assessments are included throughout the "From the Classroom" sections for whole class lessons and menu activities.

Also, a special section, "Linking Assessment with Instruction," is provided for five of the whole class lessons. These sections provide observation guidelines that relate to the specific content of the lesson and help teachers learn about individual students' spatial abilities and geometric understanding. These sections address general approaches and attitudes toward learning and comment about students' persistence, risk taking, confidence, enthusiasm, flexibility, curiosity, inventiveness, skepticism, and ability to cooperate with others.

Formal Assessment Tasks

Formal assessment tasks are specific assignments that help teachers learn about how the class in general is responding to the instruction and about what individual children understand. A formal assessment is similar to a learning activity in that it asks students to think about an issue, question, or problem. However, a formal assessment gives teachers additional information about students' understanding.

All of the five assessments listed on page 17 are formal assessments. One assessment appears at the beginning of the unit; the rest are placed throughout the second half of the unit to be completed after children have had experience with some of the ideas and activities presented.

Children shouldn't be made to feel that formal assessments are tests. For students, assessments should be the same as other activities in which they consider a mathematical idea and then describe what they understand and how they reason.

ASSESSMENT

What Is a Triangle?

This assessment helps teachers get a sense of the range and depth of students' understanding of triangles. Although students work with many different geometric shapes in this unit, the triangle is part of almost all the activities. Therefore, it's a good shape to use for this early assessment and for comparison with children's understanding after the unit.

Begin this assessment with a class discussion. Tell the students that you'd like to hear what they know about triangles. Listen to their ideas without judging or correcting.

When all interested children have reported their ideas, tell the children that you want to remember what they said, so you'd like them to describe in writing what they think a triangle is. Reassure them that there is no "right" answer by saying that they all have had different experiences and have different ideas, so they will all have different things to write.

There are ways to help all children engage in this experience, regardless of their comfort or ability with writing. Encourage children to draw pictures to help communicate. You may wish to say that spelling is less important to you than their ideas, and let them spell words the way they sound. Also, you may need to take dictation from some beginning writers. (For more information supporting beginning writers, see page 7.)

Tell the children that after they have studied shapes for a while, they will have another chance to write about triangles. Keep their papers so that you can compare them with the later assessment *What Is a Triangle? (Revisited)*. (See page 148.)

FROM THE CLASSROOM

When I told the class we were going to study different shapes, the children began looking around the room, pointing at and naming the shapes they saw. I called them to attention and said, "You sure do see a lot of shapes! But now we're going to talk about just one of those shapes—the triangle."

I then posed a question. "How would you describe a triangle to someone who has never seen one?" I asked. "For example, what if a Martian who had never seen a triangle walked into our room. How could you explain what a triangle is?"

Josie's hand waved wildly. "I know! You could draw him a triangle!"

"What would your picture look like?" I asked. Josie traced a triangle in the air.

"Can you all draw a triangle in the air?" I asked the children, checking to make sure that they had the correct shape in mind. Some children watched others draw triangles before tracing their own in the air. "Show me one more time what a triangle looks like," I said, to make sure these last children knew the shape we were discussing. They seemed to, so I continued.

"What could you say about a triangle?" I asked.

"It has three corners," Alejandra said.

"It has three lines," Stacy added.

"You could make a shape out of it," Steve told us.

"What do you mean?" I asked.

"You could draw a star with triangles," Steve explained.

"And pizza," contributed Adrian.

"You have different ways to describe triangles," I said. "I think you have different ways to talk about triangles because you've all had different experiences. I'm interested in all of your ideas. What I'd like each of you to do is write a letter to explain what a triangle is. If you like, you can write your letter to a Martian. Put all the things that are in your head about triangles onto your paper. You can draw and you can write. But you don't need to worry about spelling; just put the letters that you think might be there."

Danny commented, "If you don't know how to spell 'house,' you could just draw a little picture of a house."

"You certainly could," I said.

I wrote a prompt on the board that children could use if they wished:

> Dear Martian,
> A triangle _____

"This might help some of you get started writing," I explained.

"Who knows what to do?" I asked the children. I had four children restate the task before I let the class start working.

Observing the Children

As students began the task, Alejandra asked me, "Can I work with Stacy?"

"Not today," I answered. "You often work with partners, but today I want to see what you know by yourself."

I circulated around the room. Martha motioned me over. She had drawn a house shape with a triangle on the top and a square on the bottom. "Are you talking about the top or the bottom?" she inquired. As I pointed to the top, I wondered how many other children were equally unclear about what "triangle" meant.

Alejandra, Linda, and Alma were talking, and I wanted to refocus them on the assignment. I asked, "How would you explain what a triangle is to someone who had never seen one?"

"Pretend that you're explaining it?" Alma asked. "Oh!"

"I'd like you to start writing," I encouraged them.

The once-blank papers became covered with pictures and words. Raquel called me over to tell me a story about her picture: "There's a bike riding on a triangle, and a car seat with a baby going down the triangle hill. Then he jumped into a pool and he's floating." I asked her to write the story.

As children finished, I asked them to read to me what they had written. Some children were beginning writers. When the words they "read" to me differed markedly from the writing, I noted what the child said on a Post-It™ Note, saying, "This will help me remember." The note would jog my memory later, yet it showed respect for the child's efforts by leaving the work in its original form.

Other children were more mature writers. I occasionally pushed these children to spell more accurately or explain more clearly.

NOTE When children write in math class, it's appropriate to accept their work when they clearly communicate their thinking about the mathematics at hand. However, when students' ideas are unclear to you or you think that they could include more, you might ask them to revise or elaborate on their work. Also, in some instances, you can ask children to edit their writing to correct spelling, grammar, and punctuation errors. Deciding when to accept children's work and when to push for more requires professional judgment.

The Children's Responses

Most children's writing listed things in the world that were triangular. Danny wrote: *Dear Marshen, A triangle looks like a slice of pizza and a triangle Looks Like a triagel on your house. You can use a triagels in pool to set the balls. Juzzis [Jacuzzis] and spas look like triagles somtimes. triangels are Like boxes sometimes. triangels are Like funnules in tranadeos and typoons and Hurricens. triangels are everywhere.*

Jonathan showed the Martian how to draw a triangle.

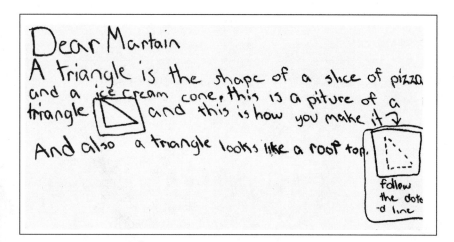

Raul wrote: *You can make a hous out of a triangle. You can make a triangle out of a star.* Then he illustrated his ideas.

Raul described objects in the world that have triangular shapes.

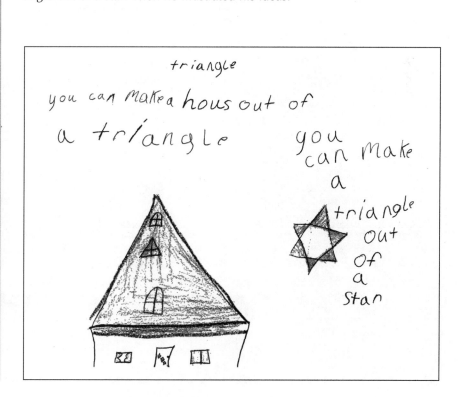

Some children described attributes of triangles. Carmen wrote: *Se acen con tes palos.* (They're made with three sticks.)

Marcos wrote: *I now about Triangles is thay are Pontey* [pointy] *and thay havie 3 sibs* [sides].

Marcos wrote about two properties of triangles and elaborated with pictures.

Alma described several attributes of triangles.

Francisca wrote: *A triangle can be roof for a house. I know that a triangle has 3 sides. And a triangle has 3 corners.*

I put the children's papers in a folder to revisit at the end of the unit.

Francisca explained what she knew about triangles and drew an illustration.

A triangle could be a roof for a house.
I Know that a triangle has 3 sides.
And a triangle has 3 corners.

look a triangle on the house

Stacy included information about other shapes as well.

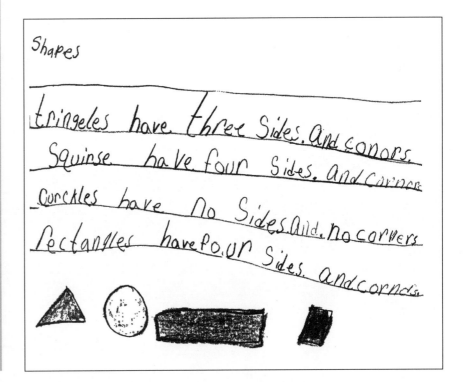

Shapes

tringeles have three Sides. And conors.
Squinse have four Sides. And corner
Curckles have no Sides. And. no corners
Rectanles have four Sides. andcornds.

CONTENTS

WHOLE CLASS LESSONS

The unit includes six whole class lessons. Each lesson introduces students to a different way of investigating shapes.

In the first lesson, *Rocket Discovery,* the children are shown a "rocket" shape and asked to construct an identical shape by cutting a square into four pieces and rearranging them. The lesson gives children experience cutting squares into other shapes and arranging the pieces to make new shapes.

Hold and Fold is the second lesson. Children make five specific folds in a paper square. They then explore the different shapes possible from refolding the square on one or more of the fold lines.

The children's book *A Cloak for the Dreamer* provides the context for the third whole class lesson. In the story, a tailor's sons learn what types of shapes sewn together work best to create a cloak to keep out the wind and rain. After hearing and discussing the story, students create patchwork designs from construction paper shapes.

In *Triangles on the Geoboard,* the fourth whole class lesson, students work in small groups to make triangles of different sizes and shapes on geoboards. The lesson also involves children in examining the properties of triangles and sorting them in several ways.

The fifth whole class lesson, *Shapes with Pattern Block Triangles,* presents children with the problem of creating shapes by arranging two, three, four, and five Pattern Block triangles.

The sixth whole class lesson, *Quilts from Nine-Patch Patterns,* is a culminating activity for the unit. Children choose a nine-patch pattern, create nine copies of it, and arrange the patterns into a 3-by-3 quilt. The lesson gives students the opportunity to examine the geometric intricacies that appear in quilts.

The lessons in the unit give children many experiences exploring shapes. They also introduce children to standard geometric vocabulary: triangle, rectangle, square, trapezoid, quadrilateral, pentagon, hexagon, parallelogram, congruent, and more.

When teaching the unit, intersperse whole class lessons with menu activities. Introducing some of the menu activities early in the unit provides students with options during later whole class instruction, when children typically finish work at different times. (See the suggested daily schedule on page 10 for one possible day-by-day plan.)

WHOLE CLASS LESSON   Rocket Discovery

Overview

In this lesson, children figure out how to cut a square into smaller pieces and then rearrange those pieces to reproduce a rocket shape. The children will probably make several attempts to construct the rocket; trial and error is a common strategy as children experiment. After the children share how they cut up their squares to make the rockets, they cut a second set of rocket pieces and explore making other shapes with them. These pieces are saved for the menu activity *Rocket Shapes*.

Before the lesson

Make a model rocket. Fold and cut a $4^{1}/_{4}$-inch square of newsprint as shown, rectangle and three triangles.

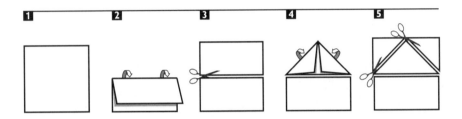

Glue the shapes onto a sheet of paper to make the rocket shape.

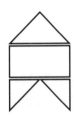

Gather these materials:
■ Five $4^{1}/_{4}$-inch squares of newsprint for each child
■ The model rocket you made
■ One $4^{1}/_{4}$-inch square of colored copier paper for each child
■ Scissors, one pair for each student
■ Glue
■ White or colored paper, one $8^{1}/_{2}$-by-11-inch sheet for each child
■ Paper clips, one for each child

Note: The $4^{1}/_{4}$-inch size was chosen because four squares can be cut from standard $8^{1}/_{2}$-by-11-inch paper.

Teaching directions

■ Show the class the rocket you made. Explain to the students that they will cut a paper square into four pieces and make a rocket the same size and shape as yours. They are to use only one $4^{1}/_{4}$-inch square for each rocket

and must use all the paper. Encourage them to experiment with different ideas, but explain that they must throw away all pieces from a try that didn't work before getting a new square. When they feel sure they've made the rocket, they are to glue it onto a sheet of paper.

■ The children work on the problem in pairs, but each child has a square with which to work.

■ Observe children as they work. Rather than guiding them or giving suggestions, focus on watching the children and trying to understand the approaches they are taking. (See "Linking Assessment with Instruction" on page 32 for guidelines on observing students as they work.)

■ Ask children who finish early to cut new paper squares and make other shapes or pictures using the same four shapes.

■ When all students have made the rocket, begin a class discussion. Ask a few children to explain to the group how they cut up the square to get the pieces needed to build the rocket. Show students how to fold the square to make the pieces they need.

■ Distribute $4\frac{1}{4}$-inch squares of colored copier paper and have the children cut them into the same four pieces. Ask them to arrange the pieces into the rocket again and then experiment to see what other shapes and pictures they can make with the same four pieces. Ask them not to glue the shapes, as they'll use them for a later activity.

■ Use paper clips to keep each student's four pieces together. Save them for the menu activity *Rocket Shapes* on page 80.

FROM THE CLASSROOM

I gathered the class on the rug and showed the children the model rocket I'd made. "All right!" "Cool!" "Can we make one too?" were the comments from the interested group.

I held up another paper square. "I cut four pieces to make my rocket from a square exactly like this one," I explained to the children.

"No way!" disagreed Steve. "Your square is too little. It couldn't make that big rocket."

Many of the students were looking at me, the puzzled expressions on their faces indicating their disbelief—or at least doubt.

"Really!" I pressed on. "I did make my rocket out of this square. You don't believe me, do you?" Some of the children shook their heads.

"Why don't you see if it's possible, then?" I continued. "I've cut plenty of squares for you to use to cut and try to make a rocket just like mine. The problem to solve is to make your rocket exactly the same size and the same shape as mine, using the whole square and not throwing any paper away."

I emphasized that they couldn't make a different-size rocket, throw away extra pieces from their square, or combine paper from two squares. "Your rocket must use all the paper in the square," I said, "and you can't add extra paper from another square."

To explain how they should work, I said, "You'll work in pairs, but you'll each have your own square of paper and should make your own rocket. Your partner might have some good ideas about cutting and arranging pieces, so be sure to talk to each other. When you feel sure you've made the rocket, glue the pieces onto a sheet of paper."

I also told the students how they could check their rockets. "I'll post my rocket at the front of the room," I said. "When you've made a rocket, bring it up and compare it with mine to be sure that it matches exactly."

I realized that trial and error would be an important part of the experience, so I added, "It's no problem if you make a mistake; just help yourself to another square. I'll put a pile of newsprint squares next to our paper supply. But be sure to throw away all the pieces from the first square so you don't get the pieces mixed up." The children seemed eager to begin.

Observing the Children

Although the children seemed to understand what to do, how to do it was a mystery to most of them—except for Elena. I heard her insistent voice behind me, "Teacher! Teacher! I know! I'll show you! I know!" She explained, "You cut the paper in two pieces and you took one part and made three triangles!" Elena pointed to the square to show where she planned to cut.

Elena quickly folded and cut apart the square into two rectangles. But when she cut a triangle from one rectangle, she ended up with a trapezoid and didn't know what to do. She tried again with the same result.

> **NOTE** Children should feel free to explore theories and experiment with ideas. Taking the view that mistakes are opportunities to learn (rather than unfortunate errors) and are part of the learning process helps to create a supportive learning environment for students.

Although Elena immediately knew how to create the rocket, actually cutting out the shapes she visualized was a challenge for her.

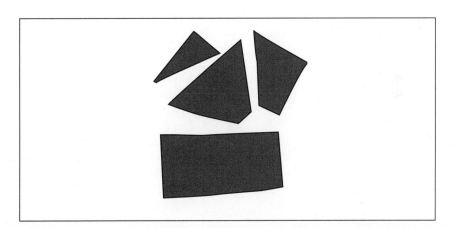

Other children did not have a clear plan, but they quickly focused on the task and began conferring and cutting. I went from table to table, watching the different ways students approached the problem.

Most children tried snipping triangles from two corners of the square. Then they looked back at the sample rocket and realized that the triangles were too small. Back to the drawing board, the children decided, and they crumpled up their first tries.

Many children first tried snipping small triangles from the corners.

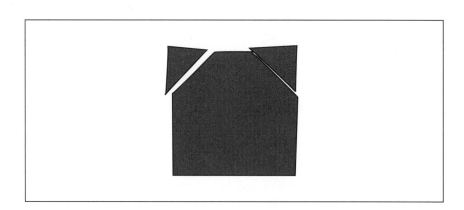

I noticed that Javier, Stacy, and Alejandra were working together and had only one paper square. I had asked the children to work in pairs but explained that each child was to make a rocket. The three children were deep in discussion; if they could maintain this involvement, I was content with their working together. I wondered how they would share the paper and make decisions. I sat down with the children to watch.

Javier was cutting apart the two rectangles. Then he and Stacy each began to argue as to who should cut out the triangles. The discussion came to a stop when Alejandra said, "Cut here and here and here, and that's how we'll get those two pieces." She picked up a rectangle and started cutting. The children began trying to fit the pieces together. I moved on.

The students in the class developed strategies and used them with varying degrees of success. Martha and her partner, Alma, took their squares up to the rocket I had posted. Martha carefully placed her square on top of the rocket and drew two lines to show where to cut. Alma realized that the rectangle wouldn't be the right size. "The other one's fatter," she said.

Amanda and Linda were watching, and they seemed to think that Martha's approach had potential. Amanda carefully measured and cut. The girls examined the rectangles and triumphantly smiled into each other's eyes, "We did it!"

Raul came up to me. "You can make it two different ways," he said.

I didn't understand what he meant. "You mean you can make the same rocket with different shapes?" I asked him.

"No," Raul quietly insisted, "there are two ways to make it."

I still didn't understand. "I want to know what you mean, Raul," I told him. "Maybe it will help if you cut it out and show me." Raul went back to his table, and I moved on to observe other children.

Raquel was confident in her initial approach to the problem. She folded the square in half to get two rectangles, one of which she set aside. Then she sat gazing at the remaining rectangle, whispering, "Three triangles. Three triangles," trying to visualize how they might emerge from that rectangle.

Raul came back to me. "Look," he explained, holding his rocket. "You can cut out one big triangle and you have two little triangles. Or you can cut two little triangles and get one big one."

"Oh," I responded, "now I see the two different ways you found to cut the triangles. Thanks for explaining, Raul. I hadn't thought of that." Raul smiled proudly.

NOTE It's important for teachers to listen to children's ideas and value their unique perspectives and discoveries. One of the delights of teaching is when students offer teachers new ideas or ways to look at a particular activity.

Elena had made the rocket correctly. I offered her an extension. "What other designs can you make using those same four pieces?" I asked. "Could you make a plane? A house? An animal? A triangle? Cut another square and see what you can come up with."

I watched Adrian and Steve confer a long time before beginning to cut. They looked at the rocket and measured it with their fingers. The two appeared very perplexed. "It doesn't fit," Adrian explained.

Then the two boys carefully cut a large triangle out of the center portion of the square. When they saw the odd-shaped piece that remained, they began to chuckle. They took another square and tried again, this time cutting a triangle from one corner, which left them with a trapezoid. They looked at each other in surprise and began to laugh. Adrian and Steve tried six times with six squares, always very surprised and amused by their results.

Next to them, Danny was hard at work refining a strategy. He placed his paper square on top of the posted rocket and traced the large triangle onto the upper middle portion of his square. His face registered surprise when his cutting produced two smaller triangles at the same time. He said excitedly, "Look! Look! The two corners that were left made these!"

I noticed that Adrian's and Steve's delight with their unsuccessful attempts seemed to be wearing a little thin. I suggested that they talk to Danny to see if he had an idea that they might use.

I walked back to Alma and Martha. They were now working separately, using different strategies. I watched Alma carefully draw lines onto the paper. When she cut the square, she found that she had a hexagon rather than the rectangle she wanted. Over and over, Alma persisted with her strategy—drawing, erasing, redrawing, cutting, and always ending up with a shape she didn't want. Her persistence impressed me.

Alma repeatedly cut the triangles from opposite corners, ending up with a hexagon instead of the rectangle she wanted.

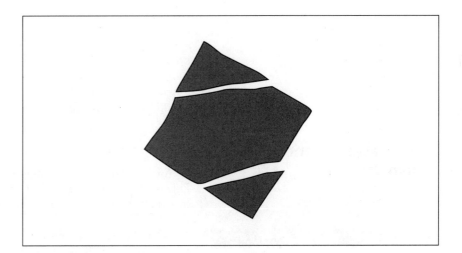

As they worked, children created and tested theories, refined techniques, and shared ideas with one another. After about half an hour, most of the children had glued-down rockets that matched mine. But a few children did not. Marcos finally asked Elena to show him how to make the rocket. And Alma was becoming frustrated that she could not cut out the rectangles. "Would you like me to show you how?" I offered. "Then you can see if you can arrange the pieces to make the rocket." It seemed appropriate to adjust the task for her so that she, too, could be successful. I offered Josie the same option. And I noticed that Martha had finally asked Stacy to show her how to make the rocket.

A Class Discussion

I held up my original 4¹/₄-inch square and asked, "What did you find out? Is it possible to make my rocket from this paper?" I was taken aback by the response: About half of the class said yes, but the rest of the children— most of whom *had* made the rocket—said no! How could this be?

Then I considered that we were facing the issue of conservation of area. Some children couldn't accept that two shapes so different in length—the square and the rocket—could be made from the same piece of paper. Even making the rocket from the square didn't convince them. I knew they'd have other experiences in this unit to help them confront this conflict.

"Can anyone explain how to make the rocket from the square?" I asked

Gabriel explained how he cut the shapes for a rocket. "I drew a line to make the rectangle, and then I cut sideways," he said.

Then Raul shared the idea he had told me, that you could either cut out the big triangle or cut out the two smaller triangles. No other children wanted to explain, so I demonstrated my method of folding the square in half and then folding down the corners to make congruent triangles. My technique surprised and pleased some children.

Then I distributed squares of colored copier paper and asked students to cut out the same rocket pieces. "Several of you aren't sure whether it's possible to make the rocket. I'd like you to try again. You can use my method or any other method you like." I explained.

I had two reasons for having the children repeat the activity. I thought the additional experience could strengthen the children's spatial skills. Also, we would use the pieces in a later activity, and I wanted them to be of sturdier, colorful paper.

I gave a final direction. "When you've made the rocket, don't glue it down," I said. "I want to collect the pieces you cut."

The children made their second rockets quickly, most using their original strategies. A few told me they used the strategy I had shared. I labeled each child's pieces, put a paper clip on them, and put them away.

NOTE Young children often do not understand, or accept, that different shapes can have the same area, especially when one is taller than the other. Children's understanding that a shape can be cut apart and the pieces rearranged into another shape without changing the area develops over time as children mature. They need repeated experiences and opportunities to talk about those experiences.

Linking assessment with instruction

NOTE Observing children at work is valuable not only for assessing their mathematical understanding but also for gaining insights into their individual approaches and attitudes toward learning.

As you observe the children work, think about the following:

■ Are any children immediately able to visualize how to cut the rocket (as Elena did)? For such children, spatial ability may be their strength. (And, as in Elena's case, their spatial abilities may surpass their numerical abilities.)

■ What strategies do the children use? In later activities, notice if children persist with similar strategies or use others. Some strategies that you might notice include the following:

Using trial and error to compare the cut shapes with the model and refining the cuts accordingly.

Measuring the shapes on the model by placing the paper square on top of the rocket model to see where the shapes might come from (as Martha did).

Visualizing how the square might be cut (as Raquel did).

Rotating or flipping the square and the pieces that were cut in order to see them from different perspectives.

Talking to others or watching how others approach the problem and building on their ideas (as Amanda and Linda did).

■ Do any children believe strongly that the longer rocket cannot be made from the shorter square? Do they maintain that belief even after making the actual rocket? These children are still developing understanding about "conservation of area." They don't yet realize that the area of the shapes isn't affected by their rearrangements.

■ What approaches and attitudes toward learning do the children exhibit? Some that are valuable for learning mathematics are:

Persistence. (Adrian and Steve cut out rocket after rocket, trying different strategies. Alma showed a lot of persistence, modifying her cutting strategy.)

Willingness to take risks.

Confidence. (Elena was sure that her strategy would work.)

Enthusiasm. (Amanda and Linda showed enthusiasm when their strategies proved successful.)

Flexibility. (Raul explained two ways to cut the triangles from the rectangle.)

Curiosity. (Steve and other puzzled children were curious to see whether it really was possible to make a rocket from the paper square.)

Inventiveness.

Skepticism: not just accepting what others say but desiring supporting evidence.

Ability to cooperate with others to solve a problem. (Javier, Stacy, and Alejandra shared and negotiated their ideas.)

Literature connections

Several children's books support the experience in *Rocket Discovery* by showing larger shapes divided into smaller shapes. Some of these books also show how those smaller shapes can be recombined to create new designs, just as students do in this activity.

As you look at the shapes in these books, you may wish to challenge the children periodically. For example, ask, "How do you know it's a triangle?" or "How is the triangle different from the square?" However, do so with a light touch.

For more information about and a synopsis of each book, see the Children's Books section on page 153.

Brian Wildsmith 1 2 3 by Brian Wildsmith

Color Zoo and *Color Farm* by Lois Ehlert

Grandfather Tang's Story by Ann Tompert

El Reino de la Geometría by Alma Flor Ada

The Tangram Magician by Lisa Campbell Ernst and Lee Ernst

WHOLE CLASS LESSON   Hold and Fold

Overview

In this lesson, students fold a square of paper in several ways, as directed by the teacher. Working in pairs, they investigate the different shapes that emerge from refolding the square on one or more of its fold lines. Then they trace all the shapes they find onto a larger sheet of paper. The shapes the class finds are traced onto a classroom chart, labeled with correct mathematical names, and used throughout the unit for reference.

Before the lesson

Gather these materials:
- One 4¼-inch square of copier paper for each child
- One 12-by-18-inch sheet of newsprint for each pair of children
- One large sheet of chart paper entitled "Geometry Words"
- One large sheet of chart paper for tracing shapes for a class record

Teaching directions

■ Give the children the following directions, one step at a time, for folding their paper squares. Fold your paper along with the children to demonstrate the directions.

   1. Fold the square in half to make a rectangle.

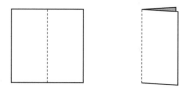

Ask: "How many sides does this shape have? How many corners? What shape do you have now?" (Record "rectangle" on the Geometry Words chart.)

2. Unfold the paper to the original square and fold two corners down to the first fold.

Explain that sometimes this is called the airplane fold. Ask: "How many sides does this shape have?" (Demonstrate how to count if the children are confused.) Ask: "How many corners?" Tell students that shapes with five sides and five corners are called pentagons. Write "pentagon" on the Geometry Words chart.

NOTE A class chart serves as a reference for the geometric terminology introduced in the unit. Eventually, the chart will list the following: rectangle, pentagon, square, hexagon, quadrilateral, congruent, triangle, parallelogram, rhombus, trapezoid, octagon, diagonal, and perhaps others. All of these words are introduced in the context of activities and reinforced throughout the unit.

3. Fold the remaining two corners using the same airplane fold.

Ask: "How many sides does this shape have? How many corners? What shape do you have now?" (Children will say they have a "square" or a "diamond," depending on how they're holding the shape. Tell them that "square" is the correct mathematical name.) Write "square" on the Geometry Words chart.

■ Have the children unfold their squares and then fold all creases in both directions to define them clearly. Tell them that these are the only fold lines they can use for this activity.

■ Introduce the investigation. Tell the children they are to find the different shapes that are possible to make when they fold the paper only along the fold lines. Explain that by "different" you mean different in size or shape. Have the children work in pairs and trace all the shapes they find onto a sheet of 12-by-18-inch newsprint.

■ Observe children as they work. Rather than guiding them or giving suggestions, focus on watching the children and trying to understand the approaches they are taking. (See "Linking Assessment with Instruction" on page 40 for guidelines on observing students as they work.)

■ When most pairs think they have found all the possibilities, call all the students together to share their findings. Post the blank sheet of chart paper. Ask a pair of children to demonstrate one shape they found by folding their square for the class. Have the others fold their squares to make the same shape. To keep an ongoing record of the shapes the children have found, trace this shape on the chart paper. Have the children count the sides and corners, then write the name of the shape next to it on the chart paper. Continue by inviting other students to demonstrate the shapes they found. Follow the same procedure for each shape. These are the nine possible shapes:

NOTE This lesson can help broaden children's view of shapes. For example, children who are familiar with Pattern Blocks may have learned that the yellow block is a hexagon. However, the hexagon they get from folding the square looks different. It's important for children to learn that not all hexagons look alike, that what makes them hexagons is that they have six sides and six corners.

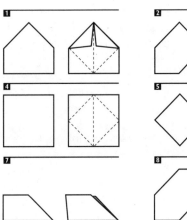
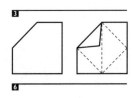
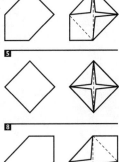

■ Have each child refold and trace all of the shapes on a new sheet of newsprint, this time labeling them with their geometric names. Students take these papers home, along with their folded squares, and work with their parents to make each shape. (See the Homework section, page 160.)

FROM THE CLASSROOM

I gave each child a 4¼-inch square of copier paper. "Watch closely," I told the children, "and fold your paper just the way I fold mine."

I folded my square in half. When the children had folded their papers, I had them count along with me to verify that there were four sides and four corners. I asked, "What shape is it?" Most of the children answered, "Rectangle," and I wrote "rectangle" on the Geometry Words class chart.

I unfolded the rectangle, refolded it in the other direction, and had the children do the same. "We want to be able to fold the paper easily back and forth, back and forth, back and forth," I explained, wiggling the fold to match my words. The children did likewise.

Now they were ready for the next step. "Next we'll fold two corners down as if to make a paper airplane," I explained. "Watch first as I do it."

There were several comments from the class. "I know how to do that!" "Look, a house!" "It's like the rocket." I find that children often spontaneously compare shapes to things in their world.

We counted and found that the shape had five sides and five corners. "It's a trapezoid," Javier said.

I didn't respond directly to Javier but explained to the class, "When a shape has five sides and five corners, it's called a pentagon." I had the children say the word as I wrote it on the chart. This word seemed to be new to the students.

I told the children to wiggle the new folds back and forth a few times, and then showed them how to fold down the remaining two corners. The resulting shape was a square, but the children had their own ideas. "It's a kite!"

"I know a game out of that."

"It's a diamond."

I held my square for the children in the position it's usually shown, resting on one side. "What is this shape?" I asked.

"It's a square," they responded.

"But I know it's a diamond," Steve insisted.

"This shape may look like a kite or a diamond when I hold it like this," I explained, rotating the shape so a corner was up. "But mathematicians would say that the shape is the same no matter how it's turned, and call it a square." The children wiggled the new folds back and forth, and I added "square" to the chart.

The children's papers were all folded. I noticed that their papers varied in precision, from Adrian's sweaty-looking, slightly irregular paper to Raul's evenly folded square. This was fine with me; the papers would serve regardless.

I went on to introduce the problem. "Today we're going to investigate the shapes you can make by folding your paper different ways. The rule is: You can fold your paper on one, two, or more folds, but only on the folds we've already made. You can't make any new folds."

I folded the four corners to make a square and continued, "You need to trace each different shape that you find." To illustrate what I meant, I traced around the square on the chalkboard. "You'll work in pairs and trace your shapes on the same sheet."

As I distributed a sheet of 12-by-18-inch newsprint to each pair, I asked, "How many different shapes do you think you'll find?"

"Six," pronounced Steve. Other children's estimates ranged from two to ten.

Observing the Children

The partners began folding their papers and tracing the shapes they found. Raul looked up and smiled. "I like tracing shapes," he said.

Danny asked me, "Can we write something in the middle?" He pointed to the pentagon he had traced.

"Like what?" I inquired.

"Like Superman," he answered. The shape reminded Danny of the symbol on Superman's shirt.

Other children chose to decorate their shapes. Some pentagons sprouted chimneys and bricks, and trapezoids grew wheels and exhaust pipes as the children related the shapes to familiar objects.

"Look! I did a pentagon," Stacy said, trying out a new word. "And upside down it looks like a cat," she added.

Alejandra and Raquel were deep in a discussion about whether two pentagons were the same or different. "They're the same," insisted Alejandra.

"No, they're not," responded Raquel. "This one is bigger and shorter. But this one is skinnier and taller. Look!" She measured one pentagon with her hand and then held her hand up to the other pentagon to prove it was shorter.

To further prove her point, Raquel placed her folded pentagon on top of the tracing to show that it matched. Next she put the folded paper on top of the other tracing. "See, it's not the same," said Raquel. Alejandra was convinced.

I walked by Gabriel and Stacy, hard at work. They had already traced six different shapes. Adrian, next to them, was also hard at work, but he was laboriously tracing his first shape. Children's abilities vary widely, yet each child can be successful with this investigation.

I watched Stacy turn her shape around and around, folding and unfolding flaps. "I can't remember where the rectangle is," she murmured. I moved away from her, leaving her to figure it out on her own.

Danny stopped me. "Can I do this one?" he asked, showing me the skinny pentagon.

"Is it different from the shapes you've found so far?" I asked.

"Yes," Danny answered, and he showed me how the two pentagons were folded differently.

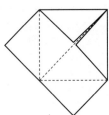 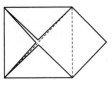

NOTE When learning new ideas, it's natural for students to try to connect the ideas to things that are familiar to them. Associating shapes with objects in their world helps children make sense of them and remember them.

I noticed that Josie and Francisca had traced two identical squares on their paper. I said, "It looks to me that you have the same shape two times."

"But we made one a square and the other a diamond," Francisca said.

"They look the same to me," I said. "They seem to be the same size and shape, but this one is turned." I pointed to the diamond. The girls agreed.

"It's okay to call it a diamond, but you need to know that the math name for this shape is 'square,' no matter which way it's placed," I explained. "Square is the mathematical name, and diamond is like a nickname."

The girls nodded. As I left, I noticed they were erasing one of the shapes.

I walked back over to Steve and Javier, who seemed to be finished. "How many different shapes did you find?" I asked them.

"Six," answered Steve. "That's how many there are." I remembered that Steve had predicted there would be six different shapes.

"How do you know there are only six?" I asked.

Steve shrugged. "We looked and we looked, and that's how many we found," he said. But Javier had just found a new shape. He showed Steve how to fold all the triangular flaps except one to get a pentagon.

Steve and Javier traced and labeled all nine shapes.

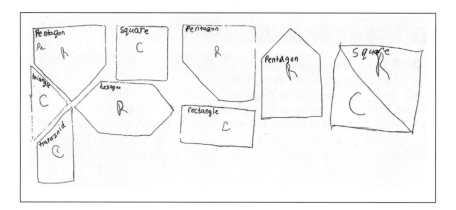

Linda was working in the reading corner and noticed the square design on a book's cover. She held up her *Hold and Fold* paper, which she had folded into a small square. "Look! It's the same!" Linda said excitedly. Then she refolded her paper into a trapezoid. "And here's that one," she said, pointing to another shape on the cover of the book.

I saw that the children had recorded in a variety of ways. Francisca had taken it upon herself to write all the names of the shapes, spelling the words to the best of her ability rather than referring to the class Geometry Words chart. She asked me what we call "that shape with five sides." Stacy had decided to write the number of sides next to each shape.

After about 20 minutes, most of the children had found all of the nine possible shapes. I asked the children to come together to share what they had discovered. I planned to give them a chance to redo their charts individually and take them home, so I didn't worry about the children who hadn't found all the shapes yet or were having difficulty. I felt a class discussion could be helpful to them, while giving the children who had finished a chance to share what they had learned.

A Class Discussion

"Who would like to come up and trace a shape onto our chart paper?" I asked, posting a blank sheet for a class record. Many children eagerly waved their hands, anxious to participate.

Javier brought his folded hexagon to our blank paper and carefully drew around it with a marker. We counted the sides and corners together.

"It's a diamond!" "It's a hexagon!" "It's a trapezoid!" the children called out.

I said, "A shape with six sides and six corners is called a 'hexagon.'" I labeled the figure accordingly and made a mental note to add "hexagon" to the Geometry Words chart. "Did you all find this hexagon?" I asked the group. The children looked at their record sheets and heads nodded.

We compared the shape with the hexagon in our Pattern Blocks. The children saw that, although our hexagon also had six sides, it was "longer," "skinnier," and "like a diamond." The Pattern Block hexagon was "fatter" and "more like a circle." I'm continually looking for opportunities for children to verbalize their ideas, to explain what they see in different ways, and to develop the language of geometry.

Adrian showed us a pentagon. The children knew it had five sides, but no one remembered the word. Francisca came close. "Pen . . . pen . . . ," she said.

"You're starting right," I said. "It's a pentagon." It would take many experiences over time for the children to learn the new terminology and become comfortable using it.

We continued tracing the figures, counting the sides and corners and labeling the shapes. The children continually related the shapes to their own experiences. Gabriel pointed to a pentagon and observed, "It looks like the face of a clown! Here's the hair." Adrian called the trapezoid a shoe. "No, it's a hat," contradicted Alma.

The children had traced all the four-sided shapes in the same area. I told them that there was a special name for all shapes with four sides. I added the label "quadrilateral."

Alejandra brought up a pentagon and began to trace it. "Is your pentagon already up here?" I asked.

Alejandra confidently answered, "No, that one's shorter." And she flipped her pentagon over to hold it against the other pentagon. It fit perfectly. Alejandra laughed and returned to her seat.

When all the children's shapes were on the chart, the children said they were convinced they'd found all the possible shapes. "That's just all there can be," was the consensus.

We talked about how the two squares in the chart were different: "One's little and the other's big."

We talked about how the three pentagons were different: "That one's fat, that one's skinny, and that one is what Superman wears."

I told the children that the chart might help them if they weren't sure of a shape's name. I thought that the children might use the chart as a resource, especially since they had participated in creating it. I added "hexagon" and "quadrilateral" to the Geometry Words chart.

Marcos held up his folded square. "Look, it's a letter," he said, and he showed me how it opened and closed like an envelope. "Can we take it home?" he asked.

"Yeah, can we? Can we?" chorused other children.

I had already planned to have the children make new charts to take home so they could work with their parents to fold the squares into the shapes. This was a wonderful opportunity to present the assignment. I assured the children that indeed they could take their shapes home. "Do you think your parents can find all the shapes that you did?" I asked.

That became the children's homework, a nice chance for them to share their knowledge and for parents to experience the geometry their children were exploring at school. Partners helped each other make duplicate record sheets so each child could take one home. I told students to label the shapes as I had done on the class chart.

For her chart to take home for homework, Alejandra chose to label the shapes in Spanish.

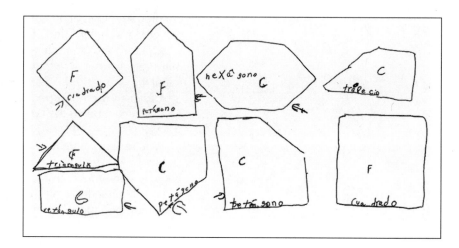

Linking assessment with instruction

As you observe the children work, think about the following:

■ Are any children especially adept at following the folding instructions (as Raul was)? Are their folds particularly precise? You will likely note broad variations in children's abilities to do this.

■ As they find shapes to trace, are any children unusually good at visualizing how to fold the paper to make a specific shape? If so, their spatial sense may be especially well developed.

■ Do any children justify why two shapes are different? (Raquel noticed properties of shapes and used this evidence to support an argument.)

■ Do any children relate shapes of things around them to the folded figures? If so, they are making connections between geometry and the world around them. (Stacy said that her pentagon looked like a cat. And Linda noticed the same shapes on a book's cover.)

■ What strategies do children use to find out whether a shape is different? Some that you may notice are:

Holding a folded paper against a traced shape to compare the shapes.

Measuring the dimensions of two traced shapes. (Raquel did this, using her hand as a measuring device.)

Making a visual comparison.

■ What approaches and attitudes toward learning do the children exhibit? Some that are valuable for learning mathematics are:

Persistence.

Willingness to take risks.

Confidence.

Enthusiasm. (Raul really seemed to enjoy this activity.)

Flexibility. (Raquel explained to Alejandra in several different ways how the shapes were different.)

Curiosity.

Inventiveness. (Danny saw the Superman symbol in a pentagon; others turned trapezoids into cars or made other associations between shapes and familiar objects.)

Skepticism.

Ability to cooperate with others to solve a problem.

Literature connections

Many children's books introduce children to the names of basic shapes. For more information about and a synopsis of each book, see the Children's Books section on page 153.

Fishy Shape Story by Joanne and David Wylie (also available in Spanish)

The Greedy Triangle by Marilyn Burns

The Secret Birthday Message by Eric Carle

The Shapes Game by Sian Tucker and Paul Rogers

WHOLE CLASS LESSON   A Cloak for the Dreamer

Overview

In this activity, the children listen to the story *A Cloak for the Dreamer*, which tells how a tailor's three sons each made cloaks by piecing together shapes. After hearing the story, the children, working in pairs, cut out shapes in two colors of construction paper and arrange them to make a design for a new cloak.

Before the lesson

Gather these materials:
- *A Cloak for the Dreamer* (See Children's Books section, page 154.)
- Tagboard shapes for tracing onto construction paper, four or five of each shape (See Blackline Masters section, page 173.)
- Construction paper in different colors
- One sheet of 12-by-18-inch white paper or newsprint for each pair of students
- Scissors
- Glue

Teaching directions

■ Read *A Cloak for the Dreamer* to the class. This children's book is a story about a tailor who receives an order from the Archduke for three cloaks to keep out the wind and the rain. He asks each of his three sons to make one of the cloaks. The oldest son cuts and sews together rectangles; the middle son uses squares and then, because he has worked so quickly, makes another with triangles; the youngest son, who dreams more of faraway places than sewing, makes a cloak by cutting and sewing together circles. The story is resolved when the father and two older sons fix the youngest son's cloak by taking it apart, cutting each circle into a hexagon, and sewing it back together.

■ Ask the class why the third son's cloak made of circles wouldn't keep out the wind and the rain. Have all students who volunteer explain their reasoning.

■ Tell the children that they are going to work in pairs to make patchwork patterns that could be used to make cloaks for the Archduke. Show the children the tagboard shapes they will use and tell them that each pair of students will choose one shape and two colors of construction paper. They will trace the shape and cut out at least four but no more than eight pieces from each color.

■ Explain to the children that they must arrange the pieces so that sides of the same length match. To demonstrate what you mean, hold two right triangles together in different ways.

These are okay:

   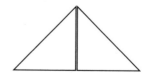

These are not okay:

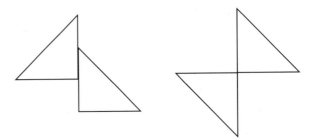

For each position, have the children tell you whether it is okay to put the shapes together that way. Tell them that when they work, all their pieces must match sides of the same length, without gaps or overlapping. Demonstrate that with two rectangles, the children can place two short sides against a long one because they match exactly.

■ Observe the children as they work. Rather than guiding the children or giving them suggestions, focus on watching them and trying to understand their approaches. (See "Linking Assessment with Instruction" on page 48 for guidelines for observing students as they work.)

■ Encourage the children to explore different arrangements before choosing one pattern to glue down. If they like, they may cut more shapes from each color to complete their design.

■ Save the children's designs to help introduce the menu activity *Cloak Patterns* on page 96.

FROM THE CLASSROOM

NOTE Probing when children respond gives them the opportunity to explore their thinking further and clarify their ideas, while helping to reveal the depth or fragility of their understanding. Asking children questions about their thinking also reinforces for them that their ideas are important.

I gathered the children on the rug and read aloud *A Cloak for the Dreamer.* The children were very interested in the story. When I read about the youngest son's problem, they immediately had some ideas that would help him.

"He should cover the circles with other circles," recommended Alejandra.

"Or put diamonds in the holes," added Amanda.

I finished reading the story and asked the children, "What was the problem with the youngest son's cloak?"

"It's got spaces between," commented Francisca.

"There are diamond holes," Carmen said.

"Why are there holes in this cloak and not in the others?" I asked, curious about how the children would explain the differences.

"Circles are round," Martha told us, and the other children nodded.

"But why are there holes with circles and not with the other shapes?" I persisted.

The children looked at each other. Gabriel attempted an explanation. "You see," he said, "circles are round and they don't have edges."

Alma added to Gabriel's idea. "They don't have corners and they don't fit together."

I gave students the assignment. "You're going to put shapes together to create a design for a cloak for the Archduke," I told the children. I explained that they would work in pairs.

"You'll use one shape for your cloak design," I explained. I showed the children the envelope that held the shapes they could trace and removed a sample of each. I had volunteers give the correct geometric names for each.

"You may choose two colors for your pattern," I explained, "and you'll need to cut four to eight shapes from each color. For example, you might cut out five green rectangles and five purple rectangles, or any two colors you'd like." I pointed to the supply of construction paper.

I traced and cut out two triangles, explaining that the triangles were the "cloth" and that we would be gluing this "cloth" to the large paper. "Try to trace the shapes in a way that uses up the least paper possible," I said as I worked.

"Working together, arrange your shapes so the sides of the same length match," I continued. I held up the two triangles in different positions, putting different sides together, always asking, "Is this okay?" or "Does this follow the rule?"

Also, I showed them how it was all right to match rectangles so that two short sides fit against one long side. "Sides must match exactly, with nothing extra," I said.

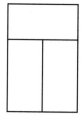

I told the children to experiment laying out their shapes in different arrangements to find the design they liked best. I placed the colored triangles on the white paper, modeling as I spoke. "The shapes have to touch each other, never overlapping and never leaving spaces in between. We want this to be a warm cloak for the Archduke," I explained.

"When you agree on a pattern," I said, "glue the shapes onto newsprint." I showed the children the 12-by-18-inch paper they were to use.

I wanted the children to understand that their cloak patterns didn't need to cover the entire paper. So I said, "If your pattern is made of ten small triangles, you'll end up with a smaller design than if you used ten large triangles. Your patterns will end up different sizes, depending on the shapes you choose and how many of each you cut out. So you'll probably have some of the newsprint showing around the edges of your design."

Observing the Children

I watched Elena and Alma choose a shape. "Let's get the big triangle," said Elena.

"But I want the little triangle," countered Alma. The girls went back and forth, unable to agree. Finally Elena convinced Alma, saying, "They're both the same, but one's just bigger." The girls took a big triangle to the table and sat down to work.

The hum of children making decisions and retrieving supplies filled the room. "Did you get the glue?" "What colors should we use?"

"Should I get two blue papers?" Raul asked me, his large square in hand. I thought he was wondering whether he needed two sheets of paper to cut out his squares. As I had him hold his square against the paper so he could visualize how much area each square required, Raquel looked over. "Ms. Confer," she said, "he means can he do all blue squares." Raul nodded. I smiled and said, "You need to use two different colors."

I watched as Elena began to trace triangles on purple paper and Alma on red. Elena glanced up at me, saying, "Look how I do this." She laid the long side of the tagboard triangle against the long side of the triangle she had just traced, and only needed to draw the two remaining sides of the triangle.

"You're using what you know about triangles to make your work go faster and to save paper," I commented. Elena advised Alma to do it the same way.

Alma and Elena decided on a pattern of purple and red triangles.

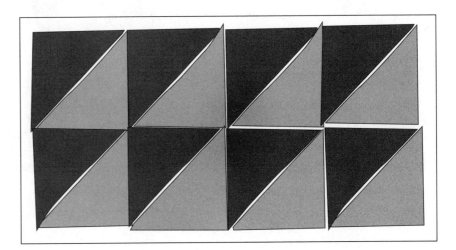

Gabriel also cut triangles. He had fit his tagboard triangle right against the corner of the construction paper and only had to draw and cut along a single line. After cutting off all four corners of his construction paper, Gabriel was left with an interesting shape. Together we counted its eight sides and eight corners, and I told him it was an octagon.

Francisca came up to me. "Can we do more than five reds?" she asked.

"Yes," I said. "You can cut up to eight of each color." Francisca skipped away.

Linda and Stacy were arranging their design of four purple squares and four red squares. "This is really fun," Linda said to me. "It's got a pattern. Red, purple, red, purple, red, purple."

"If we had another we could do this," said Stacy, arranging the squares in a three-by-three array.

"What color would you need to cut out?" I asked. Stacy answered, "Red."

Javier came up to me, asking, "Where's the glue?" I asked him to talk to his partner, Alejandra, to see if she knew. If she didn't know, I'd be glad to help. A few minutes later, there stood Alejandra. "How many colors can we use?" she asked me.

"Did you ask Javier?" I inquired. She shook her head. I want children to see their partner as the resource, to become independent of me. As Alejandra returned to her seat, I moved to the other side of the room, hoping that my distance would help.

A few minutes later, Alejandra walked across the room to ask me whether I thought the red squares should all be together. I told her again that was something she and Javier would decide. A short time later I was relieved to notice that Alejandra and Javier, their heads bowed over the paper, were deep in conversation as they developed a plan.

Alejandra and Javier's rectangles spiraled around the paper's edge, always alternating colors.

I noticed differences in how the children traced their shapes to cut them out. Francisca was careful to trace one triangle right next to another triangle, so as to fit as many as possible on the paper. After a while she didn't trace the hypotenuse of the next triangle, and merely flipped the triangle over and traced the two other sides. Her triangles made a long column down the side of the paper.

Martha, however, was tracing her triangles arbitrarily on the paper, leaving large gaps in between. I encouraged her to try to waste the least paper possible. "You could fit another triangle in that space," I said. Martha looked at me, perplexed. Although she only needed to rotate the triangle slightly, Martha didn't see how it could fit.

I said, "Turn your triangle a little." The light dawned in her eyes and Martha smiled, rotated her triangle, and traced it. I wondered if she would find this strategy useful in other circumstances.

Adrian and Steve spent a long time disagreeing about which shape they would use, who would do the tracing, and who would do the cutting. They seemed to be arguing for the sake of arguing. "You know," I interjected, "you're going to have to find a way to make your decisions or it's going to take you a long time to make your cloak designs." They glanced up at the clock. "Okay, you can cut," sighed Steve.

I watched Raquel and Jonathan working on their design made of large triangles. Jonathan was cutting triangles and Raquel was placing them on the larger paper. Raquel looked unhappy with her final triangle, which was hanging off the edge of the paper. "Raquel," I said, "there is a way for that triangle to fit." It didn't take her long to rotate the triangle and slip it in place.

Jonathan cut the cloak's triangles and Raquel arranged them.

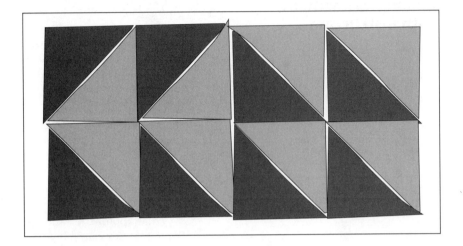

Adrian and Steve had begun arranging their squares. They were leaving large gaps between the shapes. I reminded them that the shapes must fit right against each other.

Elena and Alma were having trouble getting their right triangles to line up. "I'm trying to figure out how this goes," Alma said. I reminded them that the shapes had to be arranged so that the sides of the same length were matched.

Elena put two triangles together in different ways, and finally found a way that worked. Elena smiled at Alma, and then they arranged and rearranged their red and yellow triangles until they found a design they liked. "I'll show you something," Alma explained to me. "This is the eye, the eye, the ear, the nose, the mouth, and the eyebrows." As she said "eyebrows," she moved that triangle above the "eyes." "Nope, no spaces," Elena reminded her firmly. I left the children to continue by themselves.

Amanda and Josie's rectangles made a striped cloak.

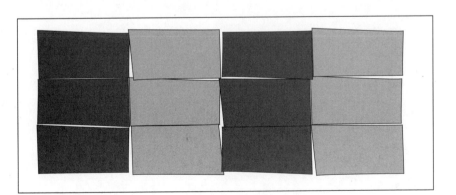

A Class Discussion

A class discussion of the patterns that the children created serves as a useful springboard to the menu activity *Cloak Patterns.* See page 97 for a description of that discussion.

Linking assessment with instruction

As you observe the children work, think about the following:

■ Do any children fit their tagboard shape right against the sides or corners of the construction paper or against sides of other shapes they have already traced (as Elena and Gabriel did)? These children are using what they know about properties of shapes to help them work more efficiently.

■ Do any children try to rotate or flip shapes in order to match sides or fit shapes within a limited area? (As Martha struggled, she was developing important spatial intuitions.)

■ Do any children try to create patterns within their cloak, or do they use shapes to create images of things around them (as Alma did)?

■ What approaches and attitudes toward learning do the children exhibit? Some that are valuable for learning mathematics are:

Persistence.

Willingness to take risks.

Confidence.

Enthusiasm. (Linda enjoyed this activity.)

Flexibility. (Stacy saw two different ways that squares could be arranged.)

Curiosity.

Inventiveness. (When Amanda and Alejandra heard about the youngest son's problem, they invented unusual solutions.)

Skepticism.

The ability to cooperate with others to solve a problem. (Alma and Elena found a way to decide which shape to use and helped each other cut out their triangles. They worked together to arrange the triangles into a design that pleased them.)

WHOLE CLASS LESSON

Triangles on the Geoboard

Overview

This two-part lesson gives children the opportunity to focus on the properties of triangles. The children create triangles on their geoboards, draw them on dot paper, and cut them out. The challenge is for each group to make eight different triangles so that none are congruent. The class sorts these triangles in different ways, according to various properties.

Before the lesson

Gather these materials:
■ One geoboard and two rubber bands for each child or pair of children
■ At least 10 sheets of geoboard dot paper for each group of four children (See Blackline Masters section, page 175.)
■ Scissors
■ Rulers

Teaching directions

Part 1: Introducing the Triangle Problem

■ Make two congruent triangles, each on a separate geoboard but in different positions and with one triangle flipped.

Ask the children to explain why the two triangles are the same. Then show how to draw the triangles on dot paper, cut them out, and compare them. Tell the students that when two shapes are the same, they're called "congruent." Add "congruent" to the class Geometry Words chart.

■ Change the triangle on each geoboard, this time making triangles that are not congruent.

 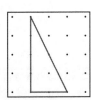

Have children explain why they're different. Again, record the triangles on dot paper, cut them out, and compare them. To check students' understanding, ask several of them to explain in their own words what "congruent" and "different" mean.

■ Direct the children to make triangles on their geoboards, draw them on dot paper, and cut them out. Tell them that they'll work in groups of four to make at least eight different triangles. If they find that two cut-out triangles are congruent, they should discard one. Suggest that when they draw on dot paper, they use a ruler so that they can connect dots with straight line segments.

■ Distribute geoboards and rubber bands to the children and 10 sheets of dot paper to each group. (You might want to have one child from each group get the materials.) Make additional dot paper available for groups that need more.

■ Observe children as they work. Rather than guiding them or giving suggestions, focus on watching the children and trying to understand the approaches they are taking. (See "Linking Assessment with Instruction" on page 57 for guidelines on observing students as they work.)

■ At the end of the period, collect the children's paper triangles. Clip together each group's triangles and label them so that later you can return them to the group.

Part 2: Sorting the Triangles

■ Return the triangles to the groups. Ask each group to choose two triangles that they think are interesting and likely to be different from other groups' triangles. Place a large sheet of paper on the rug and have the children gather around. Ask each group to place their two triangles on the paper.

■ Have the children examine the triangles to see if any are congruent. Check by matching. Ask groups to add different triangles if there are duplicates so that there are about 12 different triangles in all.

■ Ask if anyone sees any triangles that share some characteristic and could belong together. For example, a child might say, "These two are the same because they have one short side." Ask if any of the other triangles would also fit into that group. Arrange the triangles into two sets, those that have one short side and those that don't.

■ Rearrange the triangles so that they are no longer sorted into two groups. Ask the children if they see another way the triangles can be sorted. Sort the triangles into two new sets. If time and interest allow, have the children identify one more way to sort the triangles. If not, collect the remaining triangles and plan to continue sorting in a similar way at another time.

FROM THE CLASSROOM

I used one class period for Part 1 of the lesson in which the children cut out their triangles. I began class the next day by having the children "repair" their triangles. (The lines on some triangles were not straight.) Then we sorted the triangles in different ways.

Part 1: Introducing the Triangle Problem

Rather than introduce the problem with the children at their tables, I chose to gather the children on the rug so that they would be nearer to me. When the children are close together, I find it easier to pay attention to

more of them as I introduce a new activity. Also, I was going to have the students look at triangles I made on geoboards, and I felt it would be easier for them to see if they were on the rug.

"I'd like each of you to trace a triangle in the air," I said. Most children did this confidently. A few children, however, watched the others before drawing their own.

I showed the children two triangles on separate geoboards.

One triangle was a mirror image of the other. "I think these two triangles are the same," I said. "Can anyone explain why I think that?"

"One of them's facing this way and the other's facing that way," announced Raul matter-of-factly.

"I see why you think they're facing different directions," I responded, "but how are you sure they're the same size and shape?" I think it's important to push children to explain their ideas as clearly as possible.

Raul thought a minute and then said, "They both touch four pegs at the top."

"Can anyone think of another way to explain why they're the same?" I asked.

"They're the same, but just pointing different ways," Raquel told us.

"Tell us more," I prompted Raquel.

"One slanty side goes this way and the other goes that way," she said, pointing. "But they're the same anyway."

Javier had another way of looking at them. "They have the same kind of corners," he offered. He went on to explain without a prompt from me. "They're sort of square."

"If I cut these triangles from dot paper, do you think they will fit exactly on top of each other?" I asked. Most of the children thought yes, but others weren't sure. I copied both triangles onto dot paper, modeling how to count the pegs to place each correctly and make it the right size and shape. I cut out the triangles and placed one on top of the other to show the children that they matched.

"This is one way you can check to see if triangles are the same or not," I explained. "When two shapes match like this, we call them 'congruent.' These are congruent triangles because they're the same size and shape. Try saying the word 'congruent.'" The children said the word softly, in unison.

"These are congruent triangles," I said, again showing the children how I matched them.

"Congruent triangles," the children repeated.

"I'll add 'congruent' to our list of geometry words a little later," I said. "Now watch as I make new triangles on my geoboards."

NOTE Children's learning is enhanced when they have opportunities to put their thoughts into their own words. Teachers can encourage this by restating a question over and over to encourage all students to explain in their own ways, rather than accepting one child's response and continuing with something new. Also, when students hear other students' ideas, they can make connections they might not have made otherwise.

"Look at these triangles," I said, showing the children the geoboards. "Are these congruent?" I asked.

"No," said Elena. "One's skinnier and one's fatter." Other children nodded their agreement.

Danny commented, "It's a different 90-degree angle."

Even though I knew that Danny had many math experiences at home, I was surprised that he knew that terminology. I wasn't sure he understood it, however. "What's a 90-degree angle?" I asked him.

Danny explained, "It means how much room there is in the corner."

I tried to clarify "90-degree angle" for the class. "If you put the square corner of a piece of paper in this corner of the triangle, it fits just right. A 90-degree angle is a square corner." I illustrated my words by holding the corner of a piece of paper against the 90-degree angle.

Then I said, "Look for a corner in the other triangle that is just the same as the corner of my paper." I waited a moment and then held the paper against the corners in the other triangle to show that one was a 90-degree angle and the other two were not.

Danny's beginning understanding of 90-degree angles surprised me.

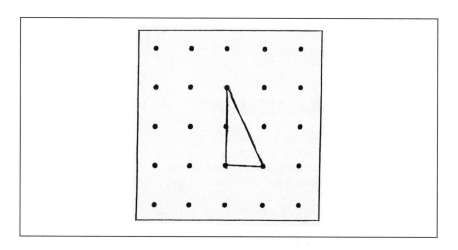

I moved on to introduce the task. "You're going to work in groups of four," I said. "Each group's job is to make a total of eight triangles. All your triangles must be different; none can be congruent."

To check that they understood so far, I asked, "How many children will work together?" The class replied, "Four."

"And how many triangles does each group need to make?" I asked. Most of the children answered "eight."

"If your group of four made eight triangles altogether, and you divided the work so you each made the same number of triangles, how many tri-

NOTE Children best learn vocabulary when it's introduced in a context and reinforced many times. By consistently using correct geometric terminology, teachers help children integrate the language into their own working vocabularies.

angles would each of you need to make?" I asked. "Talk about this with the person next to you." I presented this problem both to offer one option for how groups might work and also to engage the children in reasoning numerically. Many of the children gestured to each other as they talked. I heard murmurs of "one" and "eight" and "two." A moment later, I called the class back to attention.

"It's two," announced Raul, "because 2 and 2 and 2 and 2 make 8."

Amanda gave a similar explanation. "Everyone has to make two," she said, and she counted by twos as she held up two fingers four times to show us.

"One way for your group to work," I continued, "is for each of you to make two triangles that are not congruent, copy them onto dot paper, and cut them out. Then your group can compare your triangles by matching them as I did. Or you might want to compare triangles on your geoboards before you copy them onto dot paper. But then be sure to check the dot paper shapes. If you find two triangles that are congruent, that are exactly the same size and shape, then keep only one. Remember, your group needs to have at least eight different triangles, but it's okay to have more than eight."

I then dismissed the children to begin work. "Go to your tables and choose one person to get the geoboards and rubber bands for your group and someone else to get four sheets of dot paper. The dot paper is in the paper tray and you can get more as you need it."

Observing the Children

It took a few minutes for the children to get in their groups and get their materials. They are familiar with the routine of getting the math manipulatives from the bookshelf and paper from the tiered stack of trays.

I noticed that one group had only three children. "Do we need to make eight triangles?" asked Danny.

"Yes," I answered. "Your group does need to make eight triangles in all. So how many triangles will each person make?" I asked. I walked away, leaving the children to consider the question.

I noticed that Adrian, Javier, Steve, and Gabriel were teasing one another. They had only three cut-out triangles, so I asked, "Have you made your eight triangles? Are they all different?" Adrian hurried to make a shape on a geoboard. It was a quadrilateral. Javier intervened, "No, that's not right. Take some away, like this." And Javier reached over to help Adrian transform his shape into a triangle.

I noticed that Martha had made a trapezoid. I helped her to count the sides. She wasn't sure how to turn it into a three-sided figure. She readjusted the rubber band to change the shape, counted the sides, then changed the shape again and counted the sides. Each time, Martha found that she had made a four-sided figure. It was interesting to me how the children in a single group varied so much in their experience. While Danny had a beginning understanding of 90-degree angles, Martha struggled to make a single triangle.

It wasn't easy for Martha to make a triangle on her geoboard.

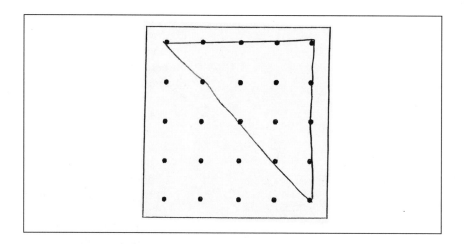

Most of the children made triangles without too much trouble. Copying the shapes onto dot paper, however, presented another problem. When Linda struggled to copy her triangle, Francisca leaned over to help her locate the dots that matched her triangle's corners.

Alma sat with a perplexed expression on her face. I noticed that she had drawn a different triangle on the dot paper than she had made on her geoboard. I asked, "Can I help you?"

Alma, a quiet child, didn't reply. I said, "I think the triangle on your geoboard is different from the triangle on your dot paper." Alma hesitated, apparently bothered by the discrepancy, but still she said nothing.

Then she erased the figure she had drawn. She redrew the triangle, this time counting geoboard pegs to guide her. Alma ended up with a mirror image of her original drawing. Dissatisfied with that, she again erased, then counted pegs and copied the triangle exactly. She smiled. I smiled as well, happy to see the persistence that Alma had demonstrated.

I looked up to see Adrian directing his group. This evidence of leadership both surprised and pleased me. "Did anyone do this one?" Adrian asked, holding up a geoboard. The group continued working in this systematic manner. A while later, I noticed that Steve had taken over the lead.

Alma struggled to transfer her geoboard triangle to dot paper, but persisted until she was successful.

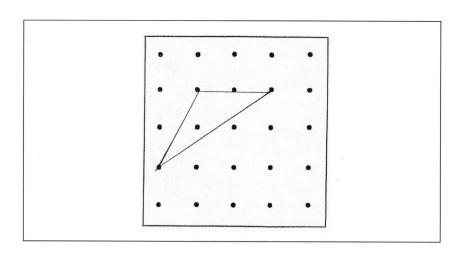

Gabriel brought his board to me. He had made a rocket-shaped penta-gon. Gabriel said that his "triangle" had three points, and he showed them to me, counting only the top corner and two bottom corners. I showed Gabriel the corners he missed, and together we counted all five.

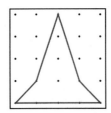

One by one, the groups told me that they were finished. "Do you have eight triangles?" I asked each group. "How have you checked to be sure the triangles are all different?" Because I want children to become inde-pendent, I require them to check their own work as much as possible.

"Do we need to make any more?" asked Martha.

"Your group needs eight," I restated, wanting her to verify for herself if the task was complete.

Martha counted the triangles, finishing with seven. "Yes!" she said, and happily got another piece of dot paper. Although I noticed Martha struggled with drawing on the dot paper, she certainly seemed to enjoy the activity.

As the groups finished, I collected their triangles and clipped them together by groups. The next day we would sort and discuss the triangles. Meanwhile, the children went to work on their menu activities. I added "congruent" to the Geometry Words chart. "You should write 'triangle' too," Amanda suggested, and I did.

Part 2: Sorting the Triangles

The next day I asked the children to get back into their groups for two rea-sons. "I noticed that some of the triangles you drew don't have straight sides," I said. "Check your triangles and use a ruler to redo the triangles that don't have straight sides. They'll be easier to compare if the sides are straight."

"Secondly," I said, "I'd like each group to choose two triangles that you think are interesting and are likely to be different from other groups' triangles." We needed a set of about 12 different triangles for our sorting activity.

The groups quickly organized themselves to decide which triangles to share. Elena held up the triangles one at a time, and the children in her group voted on their favorites. I noticed some children voting twice, but that didn't seem to bother them.

Francisca took the lead in her group. "Who wants this one?" she asked, holding up a triangle. She estimated the results. "This one is so-so," she said. The next triangle got three votes. "Are you sure? Are you really sure?" she asked the others in her authoritative way.

Other groups worked less efficiently: "Let's put up MY triangle; it's the biggest." "No, mine, because it's fattest." "Who's the oldest here?" And finally, "Eeny meeny miney mo."

When the children were ready, I placed a large sheet of butcher paper on the rug to make a work area for our sorting and had the children gather around the edge. I spread out the triangles each group had chosen.

"Are all our triangles different?" I asked. The children examined the triangles. Some hands shot up as the children detected two triangles that were the same even though they pointed in different directions. I had a student verify by matching them. One of the groups volunteered to choose a new triangle.

"Look at the triangles very carefully," I said. "We need to arrange them to show how some are the same and others are different. Talk to someone next to you and see if you notice something the same about any of the triangles."

The children clearly had ideas. Soon Adrian raised his hand. "Those are bigger," he announced, pointing to two triangles on the paper.

Danny built on Adrian's idea. "That one is big too," he said.

"Okay," I said. "Let's put the big ones in one group and the ones that aren't big in another group."

There was some discussion about whether or not some of the triangles were big. Elena resolved the problem. "Let's make a middle-size group," she said.

Danny had a different suggestion. "Let's arrange them from biggest to littlest," he said. Several other children voiced their enthusiasm for Danny's idea. I knew that arranging the triangles in size order would become problematic mathematically, but I decided to follow the children's interest. I was curious about how they would decide to order triangles—by height, area, or some other way.

I picked up two triangles from the "big" group. "Which one of these do you think is smaller?" I asked.

Several children pointed to the same triangle. "Mine's the smallest," Raul said.

"No," countered Steve, with his usual determination, "they're the same size. They're just as tall." And he counted the points that showed the triangles' altitudes, from top to bottom. Both triangles were three spaces high.

"No," Francisca disagreed, "the other is smaller. It's more skinny."

"Yeah," said Raquel, supporting Francisca's view. "That one is skinny and the other is fat."

Martha had a way to resolve the issue. "We could put all the skinny triangles together and all the fat ones on the other side." Others agreed, willing to abandon a problem and go in another direction.

"It's okay with me," I said, and the children nearest to the triangles rearranged them into two groups.

"No," said Steve, still holding onto his theory. "These two triangles are the same size. Lookit." And again Steve counted the spaces inside the triangles to show their heights were the same.

"I hear two different ways you're looking at what 'the same size' means," I said. "Steve is looking at how tall the triangles are to see if they're the same. Other people are looking at other characteristics, such as how skinny or fat they are." This seemed to satisfy Steve.

"We should organize them," announced Francisca, and she placed the skinny and fat triangles in columns, like a graph.

I asked the children to look at the arrangement. We counted the triangles in each column and talked about which group had fewer and which

had more. "How many more triangles are in the 'fat' group?" I asked. This question was fairly easy for them, especially since having the triangles in columns made it easy to compare the two groups.

The children placed Linda's triangle in the "fat triangle" group.

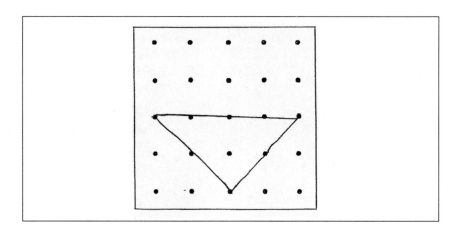

"How else can we sort the triangles?" I asked.

Gabriel had an idea: "Triangles that have three dots on a side." The children proceeded to sort the triangles.

"What are you doing?" asked Danny. "This triangle doesn't have three dots," and he moved it to the other group. As some children sorted, other children questioned and verified the decisions that were made. I found myself in the role of observer, a role that I relish because I often find that the less I involve myself, the more involved the children are.

The children finally decided that only one triangle did not have a side with three dots on it. Again we organized the groups into two columns, with one column having only one triangle. We discussed how many more were in the larger group.

At this time, I stopped the activity and collected the triangles to use another day.

Linking assessment with instruction

As the children work, think about the following:

■ Do the children have a sense of what triangles are? Are they able to create triangles fairly easily on their geoboards? You may find, for example, that some children believe a shape can only be a triangle if the "point" is up.

■ Do any children quickly recognize that two triangles are the same even when they're rotated differently or flipped? This is an indication of good spatial sense.

■ Do any children find it especially easy to copy their triangles onto dot paper? This is another indication of good spatial sense.

■ Do any children share several ideas for how to sort the triangles? They are analyzing properties of triangles and noticing relationships between

them. But don't make assumptions; even children who only seem to be watching might have noticed these relationships.

■ Do any children justify why they think a shape should go in a particular category? They are using what they notice about properties of different triangles as evidence to support an argument.

■ What approaches and attitudes toward learning do the children exhibit? Some that are valuable for learning mathematics are:

Persistence. (Alma copied her triangle over and over again until it was right.)

Willingness to take risks. (Martha, who does not often join in class discussions, offered a solution to a disagreement.)

Confidence. (Francisca was a confident leader of her group, yet I worry that her extreme confidence makes others feel less confident and less willing to join in.)

Enthusiasm.

Flexibility. (Danny encouraged the group to investigate his idea of putting the triangles in size order.)

Curiosity.

Inventiveness.

Skepticism. (Steve did not accept the other children's viewpoint that two triangles were different until the terminology was clarified to his satisfaction.)

Ability to cooperate with others to solve a problem. (The entire class cooperated well in making decisions while sorting triangles, allowing me to take on the role of observer.)

WHOLE CLASS LESSON

Shapes with Pattern Block Triangles

Overview

In this lesson, students investigate ways to combine Pattern Block triangles, following the rule that sides that touch must completely match one another. Children explore the different shapes that can be made by arranging two, three, four, and five Pattern Block triangles. The children draw the shapes on triangle paper, cut them out, and glue them onto another paper. The students discuss their findings and learn the names for the shapes.

Before the lesson

Gather these materials:
■ 10 green Pattern Block triangles for each pair of students
■ Triangle paper (See Blackline Masters section, page 177.)
■ One sheet of colored copier paper for each pair of students
■ Scissors
■ Glue

Teaching directions

■ Tell students that they will explore shapes that can be made with Pattern Block triangles. Use two triangles to demonstrate the rule they must follow: The triangles must always be put together so that sides that touch completely match one another.

This is okay:

This is not okay:

■ Use regular or overhead Pattern Blocks to demonstrate that with two triangles only one shape is possible, a parallelogram (or rhombus).

Model how to draw the shape on triangle paper and cut it out. You may also want to sketch a larger version of the shape on the chalkboard so it's easier for children to see. Add "parallelogram" and "rhombus" to the Geometry Words chart.

■ Have the children explore the shapes that are possible with three triangles. (Again there is only one possibility.)

Students should draw the shape and cut it out. Introduce the word "trapezoid" and add it to the chart.

■ Pose the problem they will investigate: What different shapes can be made with four triangles and five triangles? Remind the class that a shape is not different just because it's turned in some way or flipped over. As in previous activities, the children can test whether shapes are congruent by rotating and flipping cut-outs of the shapes to see if they match. If you think it's necessary, model this for the students by cutting out two four-triangle shapes and comparing them.

■ Observe children as they work. Rather than guiding them or giving suggestions, focus on watching the children and trying to understand the approaches they are taking. (See "Linking Assessment with Instruction" on page 68 for guidelines on observing students as they work.)

■ When the children think they have found all of the shapes, they should arrange the cut-outs on their own sheet of paper in an organized way that makes sense to them and glue the shapes in place. As children finish, ask them to post their papers for group discussion. When all papers are posted, talk about students' findings and the names for the shapes.

(Note: With four triangles, there are three possible shapes; with five triangles, there are four. Do not reveal this to the students and do not be surprised if they do not find every shape. The goal of the activity is for children to explore different arrangements of triangles.)

Shapes possible with four triangles:

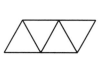

Shapes possible with five triangles:

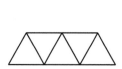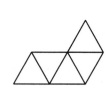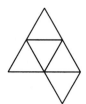

FROM THE CLASSROOM

"Today we're going to investigate the shapes that we can make when we put Pattern Block triangles together," I began the lesson. "But we have to follow one rule for putting the triangles together: Sides that touch must completely match one another. You can't have the points touching or just part of the sides touching." I held up two triangles in these two incorrect positions to illustrate my meaning. "Whole sides must touch." I adjusted my triangles accordingly.

To check that the children understood, I held up two triangles, points touching, and asked, "Is this okay?"

"No!" the children answered.

"Is this okay?" I asked as I moved the triangles so that the sides were only partially touching.

"No!" answered the children.

Then I inquired, "So how do the triangles have to be?" I called on several children to explain the rule in their own words.

"They have to touch all the way," Elena said.

"You can't have any sticking over," Gabriel offered.

Francisca told us, "They have to touch evenly."

"It has to have a whole side against it," Adrian said.

I continued introducing the problem: "When I follow the rule and put two triangles together, what do I get?" I held up the shape.

"A diamond!" several children responded.

"It looks like a kite," Raul said.

I drew the shape on the chalkboard and said, "Mathematicians have several names for this shape. They call it a 'rhombus' or a 'parallelogram.' I'll add these words to our chart. Try to say them a few times to yourself as I write them."

After I wrote the names, I clarified. "Actually, a rhombus is a special kind of parallelogram because its sides are all the same length."

"So," I continued, "do you think you can use these same two triangles, follow the rule about how they must go together, and make a shape that is different from the rhombus?"

"I can!" "Me!" the children called out confidently.

I handed the triangles to Alejandra. Her brow wrinkled as she tried and tried to make a new shape. With a confused expression on her face, she concluded, "I can't."

Raul's hand waved. He could, he was sure. Raul concentrated as he fit different sides of the triangles together. Over and over, he came up with the same rhombus. "There's no other way," he said with surprise.

To convince everyone, I held up the triangles and fit them together in different ways. "That's all there is!" was the children's verbal consensus, but their expressions told me they were not comfortable with the conclusion.

I taped a piece of triangle paper on the board and showed the children how to use the two Pattern Block triangles to trace the rhombus. I cut the rhombus out of the paper, wrote the numeral "2" on the board, and taped the rhombus below the number.

"Why do you think I wrote a 2?" I asked the class. There was silence for a moment, and then Alejandra's hand shot up.

"I know," she said, "because you used two triangles."

"You're right," I confirmed. "That's exactly why. Now, let's try three triangles. What if we put three triangles together? What different shapes could we make?"

NOTE Children become familiar with new terms and their definitions through opportunities to use them over time in the contexts of firsthand explorations. It's beneficial for teachers to model consistently correct geometric language to help students become familiar with standard mathematical terminology.

Gabriel took the triangles and fit them together to make a trapezoid.

I drew what he had made on the chalkboard for the others to see. "A hexagon," he said.

"Actually, it's not a hexagon," I said. "A hexagon has six sides and six corners. Let's count the sides and corners on your shape."

Gabriel counted them and reported there were four sides and four corners. I had the class count the sides and corners on the shape I drew to verify. "Then it's a quadrilateral, because it has four sides and four corners," I said, "and a special kind of quadrilateral called a 'trapezoid.' Practice saying these words."

"Quadrilateral" was already on the Geometry Words chart, and I added "trapezoid" while the children practiced saying both words. "Gabriel's word is already on our list," I said, pointing to it on the chart.

"It looks like a Pizza Hut sign," observed Antonio.

"Which shape looks like a Pizza Hut sign?" I asked, pushing him to use the correct name.

"The trapezoid," he said, stumbling a bit on the word.

"Would anyone else like to try to build another shape with the three triangles?" I continued. Once again, hands waved eagerly. The children seemed confident that more shapes were possible. I handed the triangles to Steve, who worked and worked. Heads obscured my view as the children around Steve watched him and gave advice. "Try this side!" "Over here." Finally Steve looked up, perplexed. "That's all there is!" he announced, handing the triangles back to me.

Again, I held up the three triangles for all to see and moved them around as the children directed. Over and over the same trapezoid emerged. I cut the trapezoid out of triangle paper, wrote "3" on the board, and taped on the trapezoid.

"How many shapes were possible for two triangles?" I asked.

"One," was the answer.

"How many shapes were possible for three triangles?"

"One," the children responded.

"So," I continued, "how many shapes do you think you could make with four triangles?" I wrote "4" on the board. They predicted 4, 7, 10, 5, and "a bunch."

"How many different shapes do you think we could make with five triangles?" I asked, writing "5" on the board. The children predicted even larger numbers. "You and your partner are going to look for all the shapes that are possible to make with four triangles and with five triangles. As you find shapes, cut them out of triangle paper. When you think you've found all the possible shapes, glue them to a sheet of colored paper in some organized way so that it's easy to see which shapes are from four triangles and which are from five."

To clarify, I said, "We already explored the shapes with two triangles and three triangles, so you don't have to do them. And remember how the triangles have to go together, with whole sides touching."

The day before, I had two children remove the triangles from our class supply of Pattern Blocks and count 10 into small plastic bowls, enough so there was one bowl for each pair of students. When I dismissed the children to begin work, I said, "Go to your tables and choose one person to get one sheet of colored paper, one sheet of triangle paper, and a bowl of Pattern Block triangles."

Observing the Children

I walked around, watching the children decide how to divide up the work. Gabriel and Steve decided that Gabriel would look for the shapes from four triangles and Steve would work with the five triangles. Jonathan and Marcos did the same, drawing a line to divide their paper, each writing his name on one section.

I noticed that Linda and Adrian were teasing each other by drawing faces. "What do you need to do?" I asked them. When the two continued the teasing, I kneeled down to look straight in their eyes, and I touched each child's arm. "You need to change what you're doing," I said. "I'll be glad to help you, but you need to get started on the activity." Linda and Adrian reluctantly began to focus on the task at hand.

Antonio and Raul had cut out the rhombus made of two triangles. I directed their attention to the chalkboard and said, "Remember, we already cut out the shapes with two and three triangles. You need to investigate the shapes that are possible with four and five triangles."

"But that's not all for three," said Raul. He continued putting three triangles together until he was satisfied that no other shapes were possible.

Gabriel came up to me, smiling, and showed me a four-triangle shape he had traced and cut out. One triangle, however, only partially touched the side of the another triangle. "We made this wrong, right?"

"Right!" I agreed. I made a suggestion: "Try building your shape on the triangle paper. That can help remind you that the sides have to touch completely."

I continued to watch as Antonio and Raul experimented with the triangles. Antonio found a shape with four triangles that he called a kite. Raul found a shape with five triangles that looked like a cat to him. "Here's the eyes, nose, and ears," he said.

Antonio looked up at me. "I don't know how to do this here," he said, pointing to the triangle paper.

I wanted Antonio to see his partner as a resource, so I said, "Maybe Raul has an idea." Raul explained to Antonio that he had to cut the same shape out of the paper. Raul returned his attention to his blocks.

"But I don't know how," persisted Antonio. Together Raul and Antonio built the shape on top of the paper. "Trace it with a pencil this way," directed Raul. As Raul's strategy became clear, Antonio smiled, "Oh, yeah!"

I glanced over at Linda and Adrian. They were bent over a shape, deep in discussion; the teasing had stopped. Then Raquel motioned me over.

Raquel had made a seven-sided shape — an irregular heptagon — using five triangles. "Is this a shape?" she asked me.

"What do you think?" I asked.

Raquel considered my question. "Well, it has corners and sides. But it's kind of weird."

"It's an unusual shape," I said. "Let's count the sides and corners." We did so. It was easy for Raquel to count the seven sides, but she wasn't sure about the corners.

"When a shape has seven sides, it's called a 'heptagon,'" I explained. "When it has a dent, like this one, it's called 'concave.' So you've made a concave heptagon." Raquel's eyes widened, and then she reached for the triangle paper to record her shape.

As I walked around the room, I heard the general hum, punctuated by children counting, "One, two, three, four, five," and general conversation such as, "Why do you like Francisca?" And Raquel sang softly as she moved her triangles around.

Elena motioned to me as I walked by. "Can't it be like that?" she pleaded as she showed me a shape that didn't follow the rule. "If it could be like that, I could find a LOT of ways!"

I noticed that two of the shapes Elena and Alejandra had built were congruent. "I see that two of your shapes are the same," I said. "See if you can find them." The girls looked and Elena pointed them out to Alejandra. Alejandra wasn't convinced.

"See," said Elena, explaining how she saw the shape. "These two triangles touch together and these two touch together and there's one left over." I had to concentrate in order to understand how Elena was looking at the shape.

But Alejandra still disagreed and tried to explain how the shapes were different. "But this has a trapezoid inside it and this one doesn't," she said.

I said, "Why don't you talk until one of you has convinced the other. Then let me know what you've decided." I left the two deep in conversation, marveling in how many different ways a single shape can be perceived and described.

I returned to Antonio and Raul, who were busy searching for a new shape with five triangles. They moved two triangles. "Oh, no! Again!" they said in dismay, as the same shape reappeared. Once again they moved the two triangles. "Again!" they said in surprise as the same shape reappeared. The children laughed and threw their hands up in the air.

Alejandra came and got me. "Look, these shapes *are* the same," she announced. "See, this is in a line and one is at the end. This one is too." And she pointed to the other shape.

Jonathan said, "Do we do six triangles?"

"Did you find all the possible shapes for four and five triangles?" I inquired.

"Yes," he answered.

"How do you know you got them all?" I asked.

"Well," explained Marcos, "we found all the shapes for four triangles and we have one more for five triangles. And since we added one more triangle, there should be one more way."

"I understand your reasoning," I answered, "but it seems to me that your new triangle can make many new shapes. See if you can find any more."

Raul patted my shoulder, "I did it! I did it! I did it!" he crowed as he showed me a new shape that he had discovered.

A Class Discussion

I asked for the children's attention. "Now we're going to do what scientists and mathematicians do—share our discoveries. What is the best way to do that?"

Jonathan said, "One person at a time can go up in front and share."

"And we can tape our papers up," added Marcos.

Gabriel and Steve began. "These are the fours," Steve said, pointing to the shapes with four triangles. "This is sort of like a triangle," he said. "And this is an 'I-don't-know.'"

"How many sides and corners does it have?" I asked. Steve and Gabriel counted and reported there were four sides and corners.

"Then you can call it a quadrilateral," I said, pointing to the word on the class chart. "That name works for all shapes with four sides and four corners. It also can be called a parallelogram."

Steve and Gabriel clearly delineated separate areas for their shapes made with four and five triangles.

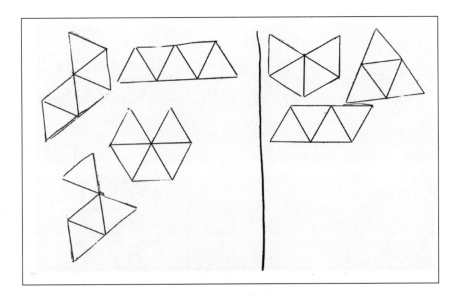

Steve continued. "This is a piece of cake with a bite taken out of it."

I asked, "Did everyone else get the piece of cake with a bite taken out of it?" Most children nodded.

"Let's count the sides and corners," I said. It was a six-sided shape. "Then it's a hexagon," I said, "but one that is different from the yellow hexagon in the Pattern Blocks."

Next, Linda and Adrian presented their findings. "We got three fours and three fives."

"Did the rest of you also find three of each shape?" I asked the children. Some children agreed, some disagreed.

When Jonathan and Marcos shared, they conferred about what to call their shapes. "This is a dinosaur's head," said Jonathan, "and this is a boat that turned over." He pointed to a shape and added, "Never mind, forget about that," as he discovered that it was a duplicate.

Jonathan and Marcos's paper showed several shape duplications.

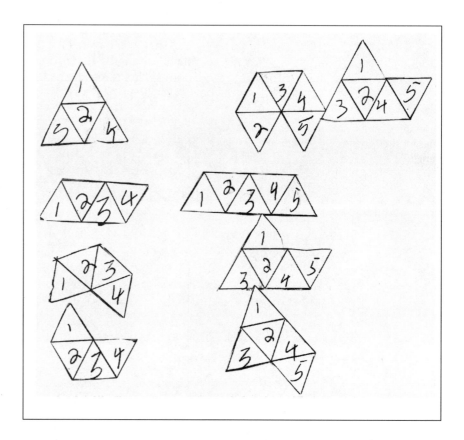

Raquel showed the shapes that she and Stacy had made with four triangles: "This is a parallelogram, this is a triangle, and this is an uncompleted hexagon."

"Mathematicians say it's a 'concave' hexagon," I offered, "because there's a part that is caved in."

Stacy shared the five-triangle shapes. "This is another uncompleted hexagon, this is a tryanchy, a pallallallagram, and a pallaguny. We made up our own names."

"How did you get those names?" I asked. Stacy showed us how the tryanchy was a large triangle with a little triangle added, so they added a little word to the big word. And the pallaguny was a parallelogram with a little triangle added to it, so they again added a little word to the big word.

NOTE Confusion with correct terminology is typical for students this age. Hearing correct language repeated in contexts of language to firsthand experiences helps children link shapes and their appropriate names.

Raquel and Stacy invented names for several irregular shapes.

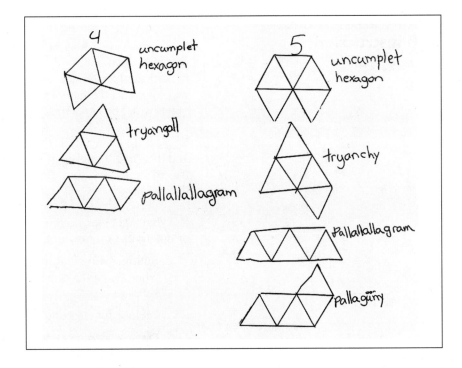

I found the children's ideas captivating, but many of the students were looking at the clock, which indicated the approach of recess. However, Antonio and Raul were very anxious to share. I wondered how best to strike a balance between honoring the children's work and accepting their limited capacity for sitting. So I told the boys that they would be the first to present their findings in our next math class.

Antonio and Raul numbered their triangles to verify how many they combined to make each shape.

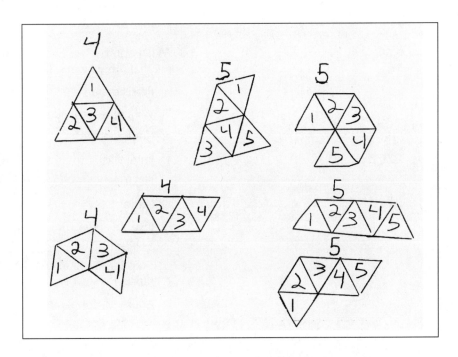

Linking assessment with instruction

As the children work, think about the following:

■ Some children may be perplexed or concerned when they find only one shape with two or three Pattern Block triangles, but others may not be surprised or particularly interested. Some children are bothered by not having an orderly way to predict the number of shapes possible with four or five triangles, while others won't be concerned. Note which children look for patterns.

■ How do the children share the work? Do they both explore four triangles and then five triangles, or does one child do four triangles and the other do five triangles? Do they organize their papers clearly so the categories are distinct?

■ What strategies do the children use to determine if shapes are the same or different? You may notice strategies such as:

Building a mental image of a shape, perhaps naming it (as Raul did when he called one shape a cat), then seeing whether the other shape is the same.

Looking for the same shapes within two larger shapes (as Alejandra did).

Placing a triangle-paper shape on top of a shape made of Pattern Blocks. The children may flip or rotate the paper shape to see whether it is the same.

■ What language do the children use to describe or name a shape? You may hear them:

Compare the shape to something in the world (such as a cat).

Describe a shape's characteristics ("that shape with five sides" or "that long skinny one").

Use correct or nearly correct geometric terminology ("a pen . . ." or "a pentagon").

■ What approaches and attitudes toward learning do the children exhibit? Some that are valuable for mathematics are:

Persistence.

Willingness to take risks.

Confidence.

Enthusiasm. (Raul was elated when he found a new shape.)

Flexibility.

Curiosity.

Inventiveness. (Raquel and Stacy created their own names for the shapes they found.)

Skepticism. (Raul continued to put three triangles together until he was satisfied that there was only one possibility.)

Ability to cooperate with others to solve a problem.

WHOLE CLASS LESSON

Culminating Activity: Quilts from Nine-Patch Patterns

Overview

In this two-part lesson, the children duplicate nine-patch patterns and examine the geometric intricacies that appear in quilts. The children examine the patchwork patterns in the book *Eight Hands Round: A Patchwork Alphabet.* Groups of four children choose a nine-patch pattern, copy it with two colors of 3-inch squares of construction paper, and glue the pattern on a 9-inch square of newsprint. Each group makes nine of these patterns and arranges them into a three-by-three quilt.

Before the lesson

Gather these materials:
■ *Eight Hands Round: A Patchwork Alphabet* (See Children's Books section, page 155.)
■ Three or four copies each of the four nine-patch patterns (See Blackline Masters section, pages 181–182.)
■ At least nine 9-inch newsprint squares for each group of four
■ 3-inch squares of construction paper in different colors
■ Scissors
■ Glue

Note: It will help the children if the 9-inch newsprint squares are prefolded into nine squares as shown.

Do this by folding the squares into thirds, opening them, and folding them into thirds the other way. It's quick and easy if you fold stacks of about eight squares at a time.

Teaching directions

Part 1: Making Nine-Patch Patterns

■ Read aloud the book *Eight Hands Round.* Talk about how the patterns in the book relate to the world in which the colonial people lived. Show the class the single patterns on each page and how the patterns combine to make entire quilts. Invite children to visualize how the quilt might look different if one or more of the patterns were rotated or turned.

■ Tell the students that they will be making quilts from paper. Show the class the four traditional nine-patch patterns from which they can choose. (See pages 181–182.) Mask off the squares that make up one of the patterns so the children can see where the "nine-patch" name comes from. Point out the shapes that were combined to make each square. Do this several times so the children can get a feel for how the patterns were made.

■ Tell the children that they will work in groups of four to create their own nine-patch patterns. They need first to choose a pattern to duplicate and then pick two colors of construction paper to use.

■ Explain that one person from each group should get the group's materials and the group's nine-patch pattern sample. Then the groups take the squares they need and cut and arrange them to duplicate the pattern they chose. Point out that, depending on the pattern they choose, they may have to cut the square in half into two rectangles, in half on the diagonal into two triangles, or on both diagonals into four small triangles. Next they glue the finished pattern on the newsprint. Each group should make nine patterns.

■ Collect the groups' patterns for Part 2 of the lesson.

Part 2: Making Quilts

■ Post three patches of each group's design side by side, edges touching completely.

■ Explain to the children that after their group completes nine patches, they must decide how to arrange the patches to make their quilt. Model how rotations sometimes change the overall design of the quilt: Remove the middle patch and then turn it 90 degrees so that different sides touch. (If you rotate a Maple Leaf patch, the design changes. This design does not have rotational symmetry. If you rotate an Ohio Star patch, the design will not change—if the children assigned colors in the traditional manner. This design has rotational symmetry.) As you model these rotations, ask the children to describe the changes they see.

■ The children work in the same groups as they did on the previous day to finish their nine patches. They decide how to arrange their patches to create a square quilt. The children then tape the patches together.

■ Post the quilts side by side. Bring the children together to enjoy the beauty of the quilts. Invite different groups to explain how they divided up the work to complete this big project.

■ Now focus the children's attention on the geometric intricacies in the quilts. Discuss the shapes that the children see. You may wish to play a guessing game. Tell the children that you see a specific shape and invite them to find that shape. Have them explain what shapes come together to make another shape (such as on the Churn Dash, where two rectangles touch and form a square).

■ Have the children imagine how the quilt would look if a certain patch were turned or "rotated." Would that change how the overall design looks for the Churn Dash pattern? Would it change the overall design for the Letter X pattern?

FROM THE CLASSROOM

Part 1: Making Nine-Patch Patterns

"Remember when we read this book?" I asked the children. I held up *Eight Hands Round: A Patchwork Alphabet,* which I had previously read to the children. I opened the book to the first pattern.

"This is the basic Anvil pattern," I reminded the children, pointing to the illustration on the left. "The other picture shows how the quilt looks when nine patches of the same design are put together."

We then looked at the Buggy Wheel pattern. "Oh, yeah, the wagon wheel," Javier remembered. Once again I showed the children both the basic pattern and the picture which showed how the quilt looks when nine Buggy Wheel patches are put together.

I told the children, "When we read the book the other day, some of you said, 'I want to do that! I want to do that!' That's what we're going to do today, make quilts out of paper. You might want to use this pattern to make your quilt," I continued, holding up the Maple Leaf pattern, which I had drawn and colored with red and yellow markers. "What does this design remind you of?" I inquired.

"A leaf. A maple leaf," said Adrian, reading the pattern's title.

"If you turn it a little to the side, it's a flower," added Josie.

"It could be a rocket," Steve said, "if you turn it upside down."

I encouraged the children to focus on the geometry of the pattern. "Do you see the nine squares that make up the pattern?" I asked. We counted the squares together. "That's why these are called 'nine-patch patterns.' Many patterns are based on nine squares. Notice that the squares are divided into even smaller shapes. How did they get this square?" I asked, covering up all squares except for one.

"They cut it in half," said Jonathan.

"Diagonally," added Danny.

"It's got two triangles," explained Francisca.

I pointed to another square. "How about this one?"

"They did the same thing—cut it in half," Amanda said.

"That's right," I said, "it's made of a red triangle and a yellow triangle."

I showed the children the square in the center of the pattern. "What did they do to make this one?" I asked.

"It's just a plain old red," Alejandra observed.

"A red what?" I asked.

"A square," a chorus of children responded.

I pointed out that the quilt had only two colors: red and yellow. Then I taped the Maple Leaf pattern on the board.

I showed the children another pattern.

"Look what she made! The Churn Dish!" said Danny. He corrected himself. "The Churn Dash."

I again related the pattern to the lives of the colonial people. "They used the churn dash to make butter. Remember that Alejandra said she'd used a churn dash to make butter in Mexico?"

"I know what the holes in the middle are for," announced Danny. "It's what you hold on to. And the other part is the sides."

Again I focused the children's attention on the geometry. "Do you see the nine squares that make up this pattern?" Then I masked off a few of the squares so the children could more easily see the smaller shapes that formed each square.

"What colors are in this pattern?" I asked. The children answered red and yellow.

"When you make your patches, you'll also use two colors," I said. Then I opened the book to the Churn Dash pattern. I wanted the children to see how the patches looked when they were all combined. "In those days, maybe one person designed a patch and his or her friends helped make other patches in the same design. Then they'd sew all the patches together. Look at the wonderful design that they got!" The children seemed impressed with the quilt.

"That's what you're going to do today," I continued. "You're going to make a nine-patch pattern out of paper, and the others in your group will make the same nine-patch pattern. You'll put nine patterns together to make a whole quilt."

Francisca had a question. "So we'll have partners?"

"Well," I said, "I thought you would work in groups of four today so it would go faster."

I showed the children the pattern called Letter X. "They should call it the Hourglass," was Javier's opinion.

I explained to the children that in the old days some people hadn't learned to write. So when they had to sign their name, they just made an "X." The idea that people couldn't write surprised the children.

Again I showed them in the book how the single patch looked and how the completed quilt might be. "But it depends," I said, "on how you rotate the patches. One might be this way and the next one could be upside down. That would make a difference in how the quilt looks. You'll have to decide how you want to rotate your patches in your own quilt."

We went on to the Ohio Star. "This is my favorite," I said, "because my family's from Ohio."

"It looks really nice when you put it together," agreed Elena. "There's a square and a triangle and a diamond."

"That's not a diamond," interrupted Danny, "that's a square. It's just turned sideways."

The children were ready to begin work. I told them the decisions they would have to make. "First," I said, "you have to choose a pattern. Second, your group must decide which two colors you'd like to use for your quilt. When your group can tell me what you've decided, I'll let you get materials and begin."

NOTE Asking children to work together in groups of four helps them learn to work cooperatively beyond collaborating in pairs. Also, some tasks are more reasonably done with four children instead of two.

Observing the Children

"What one do you want to do?" "What are the best colors?" The hubbub began as children talked and made decisions.

Javier came over to me. "Me and Danny want the Ohio Star and the others want Maple Leaf," he said.

I declined to become involved. "You need to talk to one another and explain why you want that pattern. You need to figure out a way to decide on just one pattern," I said.

One by one the groups made their decisions. When they told me, I asked them to choose one person from their group to get their materials. "How many squares will you need?" I asked one group, curious to see what they thought.

"We need more blue than red," said Adrian.

"About how many blue do you guess?" I asked.

"Maybe 40 or 50," he estimated. "And maybe 20 red."

"No," countered Francisca, "we only need 6 and 3." Francisca didn't seem to understand the instructions.

"Remember that you're going to be making nine of each patch," I said. I showed her the Churn Dash page in the book and how they had combined the patches. "Your quilt is going to be really big when it's done," I said, holding my hands apart.

I moved to Danny's group, where I saw that he and Stacy were locked in a battle of wills, while Martha and Javier looked on. Danny and Stacy could not agree on which pattern to make. "The other groups are starting," I said. "You need to make up your minds soon." And I walked away.

Adrian stopped me. "I don't get it," he said. To give more concrete directions, I showed Francisca and her group nine newsprint squares that would form the base of each patch. "This will be Raul's patch, this will be Adrian's patch, this is Amanda's, and this is yours," I said. "You'll each make the same decision. Then you'll have to decide how to work together so you can make nine altogether for your big quilt." I placed the newsprint squares three across and three down.

I saw that Raquel had already cut and glued her construction paper squares, completing an Ohio Star patch. "Yes!" she said excitedly.

Jonathan's group had formed an assembly line, Steve cutting out the red triangles, Elena the blue triangles, Gabriel the blue squares, and Jonathan the red squares. I wondered if they were cutting out the right proportions of each.

Then Elena said, "We only need nine red ones for the middle." She *was* keeping track.

Jonathan was experimenting, laying his squares out flat on the table, and then piling the same squares up, one on top of the other. He told me, "If you put the squares flat it's not much, but if you pile them it gets taller."

I surveyed the room. In all the other groups the children were working on their patches individually. After completing one patch, they moved on to another. I saw that Stacy and Danny must have come to some consensus, as their group was hard at work.

Francisca's group was ready to arrange the shapes. She began organizing them. "Look guys," she said, "we're going to do it this way." And she began laying the shapes on the newsprint base.

Adrian protested. "No!" Then he asked, "Are you doing the top part or the bottom part?"

"Oh," said Francisca, as she recognized her error. She rearranged two of her triangles.

Then Francisca held up a square that hadn't been cut very carefully. She turned to Raul and stated, "You're not cutting them right." Raul picked up the scissors and Amanda checked to see if some of his shapes needed to be trimmed.

"Now we're doing the bottom," directed Francisca. I wanted to see other children participate more, so I intervened.

"Is there a way Amanda can help?" I asked. "Let's make sure that everybody gets to help make decisions."

I watched Gabriel struggle to make his patch look like the Maple Leaf pattern. He had reversed the tip. I pointed out how the bottom matched the design. "But the top part has something wrong with it," I said. When he still couldn't see the error, I helped him remove a triangle. "This one needs to be rotated differently," I said.

I was surprised to see Elena was having trouble with her Maple Leaf. "You cut out a rectangle," I said, "but I don't see any rectangles on your pattern." After I said that I wondered if I should have let her struggle more. She might have figured it out herself.

I looked around the room. Some groups were working quietly. Amanda's group was singing some songs from the movie *Aladdin* as they worked.

I heard Francisca speaking impatiently. "You guys have to help!"

"You won't let us!" countered Adrian. He was right.

I reinforced Adrian's statement. "Francisca, Adrian's saying that he'd like to help more. Is there a way more people can be involved?"

"We need nine of these," Francisca said.

"But," countered Adrian, "do we have to finish a whole one first?" I was glad that Francisca was getting challenged for her bossiness. And the fact that her friends were questioning it was even more powerful than my doing so alone.

Elena showed me her patch. "Lookit!" she said.

"How do you know it's right?" I asked her. I wanted Elena to be able to verify for herself that it was correct.

Elena showed me the two blue triangles on the side on both the pattern and her patch. "And they both have three red ones in the middle," she told me.

I walked past Martha. She had labeled her pattern and her block with letters: "R" for red and "B" for blue. "So I know what color to cut," Martha explained to me. This was evidence to me that Martha was growing in her ability to use strategies to solve problems.

Part 2: Making the Quilts

Gabriel's group had made three Maple Leaf patterns the day before. I posted them in a row, sides touching.

"They look really good," Stacy said. I agreed.

"Gabriel's group has finished three patches," I told the class. "They will need to have nine. How many more do they need to make?" I asked. Some children's hands shot up immediately; other children used their fingers to count.

"They need six more," Elena told me.

"How did you get six?" I asked her.

"I went 1, 2, 3," she said, pointing to each patch on the board, "and then 4, 5, 6, 7, 8, 9," she told the class, putting up a finger for each number.

"6 and 3 make 9," Jonathan explained.

"When Gabriel's group has finished all nine patches," I went on, "they have to decide how to arrange their patches to make a square quilt. One thing they'll need to think about is how they want to rotate each patch."

I pointed to the middle patch. "They might want to have the patches all face the same way, as you see here. Or, they might decide to turn the patch a different way." I removed the center patch and rotated it so that different sides touched.

"It's upside down," Francisca commented.

"Now it looks like a rocket," Adrian said.

"Rotating this patch does make the quilt look different," I said.

I taped up three Ohio Star patches. "I wonder what would happen if this group decided to rotate the center patch," I said. "I'd like you to visualize, or imagine, what would happen to the quilt if we rotated this patch." I paused a moment to let the children do so.

"It would look the same," Elena said.

"Nuh-uh," countered Danny. "It would so change. The star would be sideways."

Elena tried to support her belief. "The top would be sideways but it's the same as the side. You couldn't tell." Danny shook his head doggedly.

"Would you like to rotate it and see?" I asked him. Danny removed the center patch, turned it, and replaced it.

"See, it's the same!" Elena said.

"Well, it's kind of the same," Danny admitted, "but this triangle's a little bigger."

"But the overall design doesn't change, like the Maple Leaf did," I said. "This design has 'rotational symmetry.' No matter how you turn it, you get the same design.

"You'll have to experiment with rotating your patches," I continued. "See if your design changes and decide which arrangement you like best." The children joined their groups and resumed working on their patches.

Javier called me. "Ms. Confer, do you like mine?" he asked.

"Oh," I smiled. "What do you think? That's the important thing."

"Can we do a raffle on who takes it home?" he asked.

"Sure," I said, "after we've enjoyed them in the room for a while."

I watched Raul, deep in thought as he considered a triangle he had just glued down. "Oh, I did it wrong," Raul frowned. "No," he suddenly said, holding the pattern next to his patch, "it's fine!"

The noise level in the room seemed reasonable and purposeful, as children cut, glued, compared their work with the patterns, and talked to one another. Before long, Francisca, Adrian, Raul, and Amanda had finished all nine of their patches. For once, Francisca watched, as Amanda and Adrian arranged the patches. They put four in a row, and then four in a row beneath. "What do we do with this?" asked Adrian, holding the remaining patch.

"It has to be a square quilt," Francisca announced.

"We know," said Amanda, and she rearranged the patches into three rows of three.

"But how should we turn it?" asked Francisca, as she rotated different patches. Amanda and Adrian leaned over to help. The group seemed to be working together much better today, I noticed.

Raul watched the children rotate patches. "It doesn't matter," he said. "It doesn't change."

"Yeah," agreed Francisca, "but we didn't cut so even and they don't fit the same."

After the children finished arranging and taping their quilts together, they posted their quilts on the board. Then I encouraged them to revisit a menu activity. Francisca and Amanda decided to use their rocket shapes to make new pictures. Adrian and Raul decided to look for new shapes that could be made with six squares.

When all the quilts were finished, I posted them and called the class together for a group discussion. First we admired the quilts. Then I had several groups explain how they divided up the work to make their quilts. To focus the class on the geometric shapes, I initiated a guessing game. "I see a rectangle," I said, and students told where I could be looking. I did this for other shapes as well—parallelogram, trapezoid, and hexagon.

For days afterward, children continued to examine and comment on the quilts. They were very pleased with their accomplishments.

The children completed a variety of quilt patterns.

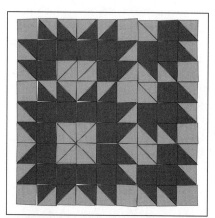

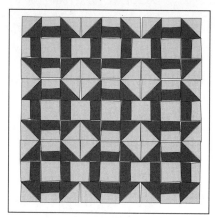

Literature connections

Below is a list of children's books that highlight the historical and social aspects of quilting. (For more information and a synopsis of each book, see the Children's Books section, page 153.)

Sam Johnson and the Blue Ribbon Quilt by Lisa Campbell Ernst

The Keeping Quilt by Patricia Polacco

The Josefina Story Quilt by Eleanor Coerr

Texas Star by Barbara Hancock Cole

The Patchwork Quilt by Valerie Flournoy

CONTENTS

MENU ACTIVITIES

The activities on the menu were selected to offer children a variety of ways to think about geometric ideas. The menu was constructed with the consideration that not all children engage with or experience concepts in the same way; it includes activities that appeal to different interests and aptitudes.

The menu serves several purposes. First of all, the menu activities offer children ways to extend their experiences with whole class lessons:

> *Rocket Shapes* and *Square Designs* extend the *Rocket Discovery* lesson.

> *Cloak Patterns* and *Nine-Patch Patterns* extend the *A Cloak for the Dreamer* lesson.

> *More Shapes on the Geoboard* extends the *Triangles on the Geoboard* lesson.

> *Shapes with Six Green Triangles* and *Shapes with Six Squares* extend the *Shapes with Pattern Block Triangles* lesson.

The menu also solves the classroom problem of students who finish activities more quickly than others. For example, in Part 1 of the whole class lesson *Triangles on the Geoboard*, as groups finish making their eight triangles, the children can choose a menu activity. In this way, they stay meaningfully engaged with the mathematics of the unit even though they have completed the requirement for the whole class lesson.

In addition, the menu benefits students by providing a structure for independent learning. Once students are familiar with several menu activities, they can work on different activities during the same math period and can work at their own pace. In this way, the menu gives students control over their learning and helps them learn to make choices and manage their time.

The menu also benefits teachers. When children are working independently, the teacher doesn't have the major responsibility for leading a lesson. Instead, he or she can work with individuals, pairs, or small groups and initiate discussions that give valuable insights into students' thinking, reasoning, and understanding.

The Importance of Class Discussions

While the menu activities provide children experience with geometric ideas, class discussions are essential for cementing and furthering student learning. Class discussions help students express their ideas, hear the ideas of others, and develop and strengthen their understanding. These discussions also provide teachers with opportunities to receive feedback about activities and assess what students have learned.

A class discussion is most beneficial after students have had time to interact with a menu activity and engage with the geometric ideas. The "From the Classroom" section for each menu activity contains valuable suggestions for leading class discussions. The situations described in these sections will not be the same in other classrooms, but they are representative of what typically occurs, and the teacher's responses are useful models for working with students during menu time.

Classroom Suggestions

The "Notes About Classroom Organization" section on pages 7–9 provides information about organizing the classroom for menus. Following are additional suggestions.

The menu activities relate to previous instruction in whole class lessons, so students are somewhat prepared for them. However, you need to introduce menu activities carefully so that children understand what you are asking them to do. When children are clear about what is expected of them, they're more able to function as independent learners. Specific teaching directions are provided in the "Getting Started" section of each menu activity.

Also, it's best to introduce activities just one or two at a time during the unit. The suggested daily schedule section on pages 10–13 offers one plan for introducing menu activities and structuring menu time for the unit.

Giving clear directions is not sufficient for helping children learn to work independently. Additional time and attention are required. For example, menu activities that require students to work in pairs are marked with a "P" in the upper right-hand corner; those that can be done individually are marked with an "I." Children might need to be reminded from time to time that information about a menu activity is available on the written menu tasks. Also, you might need to review directions several times on different days to be sure that children understand and remember what to do.

Providing Ongoing Support

You may find it useful at times to offer children more concrete models of an activity. For example, *Square Designs* asks children to write about how they cut a square to make one of three designs. After some children have completed this part of the assignment, you might invite two or three children who have successfully completed the work to read their papers to the class. Examples of acceptable work can help others who haven't yet completed the assignment. Be careful, however, to choose only work that offers positive models so that no child's work is used as a negative example.

At other times, before having the children begin work on menu activities, you might want to have a discussion about working with partners. Have the children talk about how they are helpful to each other. Ask them to bring up problems they've encountered and either describe how they resolved them or ask the class for suggestions. You may want to report what you've observed about children working independently and cooperatively. These discussions are invaluable for helping students learn to be productive learners.

Although students are encouraged to make choices and pursue activities of interest to them during menu time, they also should be required to at least *try* all of the menu activities. Be aware, however, that children will respond differently to activities. Not all children get the same value out of the same experiences; students will engage fully with some activities and superficially with others. This is to be expected and respected. Also, each activity can be revisited several times, and the menu gives children the opportunity to return to those activities that especially interest them.

MENU ACTIVITY

Overview

Rocket Shapes

In this activity, children use the same pieces they cut to make the rocket in *Rocket Discovery*, a rectangle and three triangles. They arrange these four shapes to construct a square, a triangle, a rectangle, and a hexagon. The children record their shapes by tracing the pieces. When students finish creating these shapes, they create other shapes of their own choosing.

167

Rocket Shapes

You need: Four paper pieces, the same as for the rocket lesson

1. Use all four pieces to make each of these shapes: square, triangle, rectangle, hexagon.

2. Trace around each piece to show how you put the pieces together to make each shape. Label the four shapes you make.

3. Create a shape of your own with all four pieces. On a separate sheet of paper, trace just its outline, not the outline of each piece. Put your name on your shape and post it. If you want, make other shapes.

4. Try to fit your four puzzle pieces into other students' shapes. When you do so, sign your name on the back of the paper that shows the shape.

From *Math By All Means: Geometry, Grade 2*   ©1994 Math Solutions Publications

Before the lesson

Gather these materials:
■ The four pieces each child cut from colored copier paper at the end of the whole class lesson *Rocket Discovery* (See pages 27–33.)
■ Blackline master of menu activity, page 167

Getting started

■ Remind the children of the rockets they made during *Rocket Discovery* and show the four pieces they cut from squares to make their rockets.

■ Tell students that they will use the same four puzzle pieces to make four new shapes: a square, a triangle, a rectangle, and a hexagon. Draw these shapes on the board and label them.

  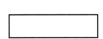

■ Explain that after they create each shape, they trace around the pieces on a sheet of paper to show how they fit together and then label the shape. Demonstrate for the class.

■ Tell the children that after they've created and traced the four shapes, they can make puzzles of their own. For each puzzle, they make a shape with the four puzzle pieces and trace just around the outside of the shape so that others can't tell how the shape was made. Show students where to post their new shapes. Suggest that they try to solve one another's puzzles by figuring out how to fit in the puzzle pieces.

■ Explain that students don't have to do all the shapes in order, nor do they have to find all the shapes in one day. If they find a shape particularly tricky, they might want to think about it overnight or save it for another day. Here are the solutions:

  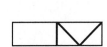

■ In a later class discussion, invite a few children to explain how they placed the puzzle pieces to make a shape. As they describe how to place the four small pieces, follow their directions, doing what they say in a very literal manner. For example, if a child says to put the triangle by the rectangle, place it a few inches away from the rectangle. The child will probably object, perhaps saying, "No, that's not what I mean; put it right against the rectangle on the other side." This will help the children refine their language and use more specific terminology.

FROM THE CLASSROOM

I gathered the children on the rug and posted the directions for this activity.

"Will you be working by yourself or with your partner?" I asked. The children knew that the "P" meant it was a partner activity.

"Remember the rocket you made the other day?" I asked the children. I showed them the colored paper shapes they had cut out at the end of the *Rocket Discovery* whole class lesson.

"What shape did you start with?" I asked. The children answered "square" in unison.

"Into how many pieces did you cut the square in order to make the rocket?" I asked. The children answered "four," and I asked for volunteers to name the shapes of the pieces.

"In this activity," I said, "you'll use the same four pieces and put them together like puzzle pieces to make other shapes. One of the shapes you'll make is a square. Do you think you can do that?"

A few children's expressions said, "Of course, Ms. Confer, we cut them out of a square, so they can go back into a square," but many children were looking at the shapes quizzically. Children vary a great deal in spatial understanding.

"Follow along as I read the instructions," I said. I read the first step: "*Use all four pieces to make each of these shapes: square, triangle, rectangle, hexagon.*"

"What does a triangle look like?" I asked the children.

"It has three sides," Stacy told us.

"And three points," Javier added.

I drew a triangle on the board and wrote the word "triangle." I purposely drew the triangle with one of the corners pointing down. Many children believe that a triangle has to be drawn with one vertex pointing up, and I wanted to avoid contributing to that misconception. No one commented.

"What about a square?" I asked. "What does it look like?" Again a few children described the shape and told me how to draw it. We did the same for the rectangle, but when I asked about a hexagon, no one volunteered.

"It's a shape with six sides and six corners," I said. I drew a hexagon and had the children count its sides and corners. Then I labeled it.

Next, I read the second step in the instructions: "*Trace around each piece to show how you put the pieces together to make each shape. Label the four shapes you make.*" I demonstrated on the board by tracing each piece of the rocket shape from the whole class lesson.

Then I read step three: "*Create a shape of your own with all four pieces. On a separate sheet of paper, trace just its outline, not the outline of each piece. Put your name on your shape and post it. If you want, make other shapes.*"

I read step four to explain that the shapes students created would be puzzles for other students to solve. "*Try to fit your four puzzle pieces into other students' shapes. When you do so, sign your name on the back of the paper that shows the shape.*"

"Be sure to put each new shape on a separate sheet of paper," I added, "so other students can try to fit their four pieces into your shape."

I introduced another menu activity, *Square Designs*, and then had the children choose one to try.

NOTE When working on the menu, children enjoy making decisions about which activity to do. Opportunities to make decisions gives students some control over their learning and encourages investment in their own work. Also, making choices helps children learn about their particular mathematical interests.

Observing the Children

As the students began working, I noticed Raquel tracing the large triangle. "You need to make a triangle using all four of the shapes," I told her.

"Oh!" she said, eyes widening. I wondered if I had made that clear to the group. They'd let me know soon enough, I decided.

Francisca and Amanda were partners, and I noticed that they worked independently of each other, yet side by side. It didn't take Francisca long to make the square. Then she began to work on the triangle. She placed the large triangle above the rectangle, and seemed pleased that the edges matched. She then placed the two small triangles against the sides of the rectangle. The edges didn't match up.

"Is this okay?" Francisca asked me hopefully.

"How many sides does a triangle have?" I asked her.

Francisca answered, "Three." Together we counted 11 sides.

Francisca abandoned her search to make the triangle and referred to her instruction sheet to see what else to do. "What's a rectangle?" she asked Elena. I wondered why she didn't ask Amanda.

Elena answered, "It's a long, stretched-out square." I was glad to see Francisca use Elena as a resource instead of turning to me for help. I wouldn't have given the same description that Elena had, and I considered how often children communicate ideas to one another better than a teacher might.

As I walked away, I heard Francisca say elatedly, "I did a hexagon!" Then I heard her sing to Amanda, "I did a hexagon, I did a hexagon, nyah, nyah, nyah, nyah, nyah." This was not how I wanted partners to work together.

I asked Francisca to come talk to me. I explained that partners were supposed to help each other. She might have some ideas for Amanda, and Amanda might be able to help her with the triangle. "How do you know it's a hexagon?" I asked Francisca, changing the subject.

"It's got six sides," she told me. Francisca sat down, and I noticed her struggle to fit the hexagon on the same page where she had traced her square.

"Do we have to do them all?" asked Jonathan. He and Gabriel had completed the square and were working to find the triangle.

Some shapes were easier for the children to make than others. I wanted somehow to maintain the challenge yet keep the children from too much frustration.

"Before you go on to the next menu item," I answered the boys, "you need to find at least two of the shapes. But sometime I'd like you to go back to this activity and try the other two. Eventually I hope you make all four."

Alejandra came up to me. "Will you do the triangle for me?" she asked. I declined. "What does your partner think about it?" I asked.

"She doesn't know," she answered.

"Why don't you sleep on it?" I suggested. "Maybe tomorrow it will become clear to you."

The next day Alejandra came bouncing into the classroom. "Ms. Confer, I found it!" she proudly announced.

"How did you figure it out?" I asked her.

"It just came to me when I was brushing my teeth. Look!" she said, showing me her tracing.

NOTE At times, children feel frustrated and want an immediate answer to a problem. Telling the answer, however, can eliminate the challenge and give the false notion that all problems have immediate solutions. However, it's also important not to increase students' frustration to the point of losing interest or willingness to stay involved. Deciding when to give answers depends on the individual child and the task.

Alejandra couldn't figure out how to arrange the pieces to make the triangle. Later that night, while brushing her teeth, the solution came to her.

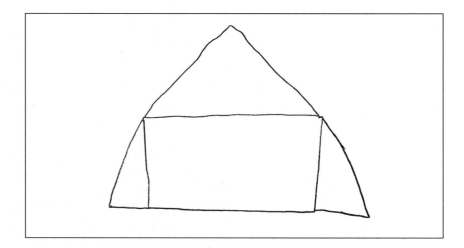

In this instance, I was pleased that I'd made the decision that I had.

I didn't initiate a formal class discussion about this activity until three days after I had given the directions. I wanted to give the children time to make all four shapes and try one another's puzzles. During the unit, I periodically reminded the children of the challenges. "How many of you found the hexagon?" I would ask. Or "Is it *really* possible to make a triangle using all four shapes?"

A Class Discussion

"Were all the shapes easy or were any hard?" I asked the class. Raul rolled his eyes. "The triangle was really hard," he said.

"The square was easy," offered Elena. "We did it before."

"What do you mean?" I asked.

"Oh," said Elena, "that's how we got the rocket." Elena had made an important connection between the activities.

Elena, a spatially adept child, easily arranged the pieces into a square. She remembered how she had cut a square apart to make those pieces.

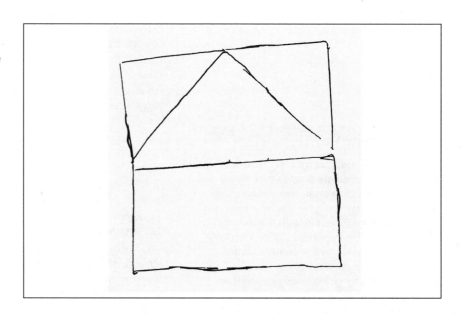

Steve and Adrian wanted to share how they had found the triangle. "I used the big triangle, the little triangles and the rectangle," Steve explained.

"How did you put the pieces together?" I probed, holding up a set of the four pieces.

"That one goes in the middle," said Steve, pointing to a shape.

"Which one? What's its name?" I asked. The class supplied "rectangle." I taped the rectangle on the board, vertically.

"No," interjected Steve impatiently, "it goes the other way!" His hand motioned sideways.

"Oh," I said, "you want the rectangle to be horizontal." I taped the rectangle horizontally. "Now what?" I asked.

"You need the big triangle," Adrian said. "It goes on the top." As I moved the large triangle toward the top, angle aiming downward, Adrian hastily added, "You have to turn it. It needs to point up."

Steve gave the last instruction. "Just put the little triangles on the sides," he said. I did so, placing the long side of each triangle against the rectangle's sides. Steve seemed content with the 11-sided figure we had created. I paused, wondering whether anyone in the class would object.

Steve tried to form a triangle with his shapes, but instead ended up with an 11-sided figure.

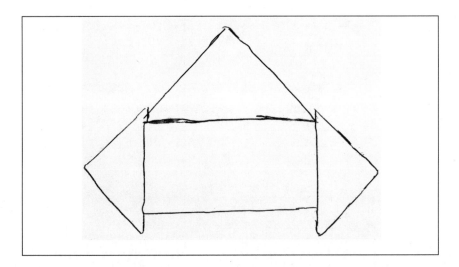

"Can I do the hexagon?" asked Francisca.

"Wait a minute," I said to the children, refocusing their attention on the shape I had made on the board. "This isn't a triangle."

"No," said Danny. "You have to turn the little triangles around."

"How can you prove that my shape is not a triangle?" I asked.

"It's got too many sides," Danny explained. "You need three." I rotated the smaller triangles and taped them to the rectangle correctly.

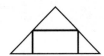

"Did anyone make the triangle in a different way?" Some children shook their heads immediately; others checked their recording sheets first.

Then I had Francisca and Amanda report how they made the hexagon. They told me how to arrange the shapes. "Put the little triangles together," Francisca said. I did so, joining the long sides.

"No," smiled Francisca, "the other way."

"What other way?" I asked.

"Use the other side," she said.

"Oh," I answered, "you want me to join two short sides?" Francisca nodded. I adjusted the pieces.

It was Amanda's turn. "You have to put the rectangle on the bottom," she said, "with the long side touching." I followed the instructions.

Amanda explained to the class how she made the hexagon.

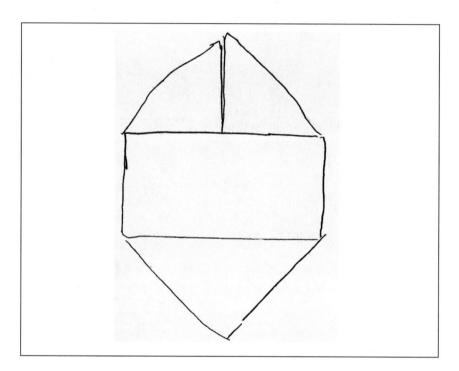

Francisca said, "Now you need the big one."

"What big one?" I asked.

"The big triangle," she said. "Put it on the bottom, but turn it pointing down."

I did so, turning the triangle so a 45-degree angle was pointing down. "Not that point," explained Francisca. "The fat one."

I adjusted the triangle. "I see what you mean. Now we have our hexagon."

"Did anyone make the hexagon in a different way?" I asked.

"I did," offered Raul, but he looked again at his paper. "I think it's the same, but turned around." He rotated his paper so his vertical hexagon pointed instead to the sides.

It was time for lunch, and I stopped the discussion.

Raul fit the pieces together to make a square.

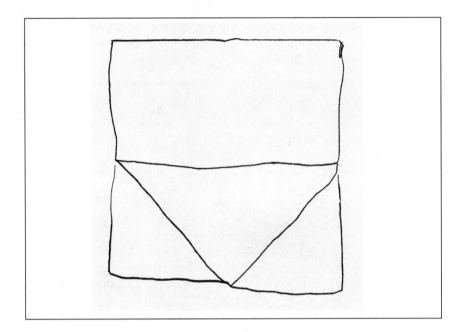

MENU ACTIVITY

Overview

Square Designs

This activity provides children additional experience with developing and honing their spatial skills by having them visualize, cut, and rearrange shapes. The children explore how to cut $4\frac{1}{4}$-inch squares and arrange the pieces to duplicate three other shapes. After they create each shape, students glue the pieces onto another paper. Finally, children choose one shape and write about how they cut the square and arranged the pieces.

168

Square Designs

You need: 4 1/4-inch newsprint squares
            Scissors
            Glue
            White or colored paper

1. Choose design A, B, or C.

2. Cut your paper square into four pieces and put them together into the exact same size and shape as the design you picked. (You might need to try several times.)

3. Glue your design onto white paper.

4. Follow steps 1, 2, and 3 for the other two designs.

5. Choose one of your three designs. Write about how you cut your square to make that design.

Before the lesson

Gather these materials:

■ Newsprint samples of shapes A, B, and C, each cut from a $4\frac{1}{4}$-inch square of newsprint as shown and glued on a sheet of paper.

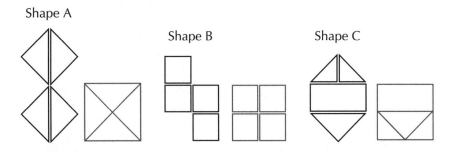

Shape A

Shape B

Shape C

■ Eight $4\frac{1}{4}$-inch squares of newsprint for each pair of students
■ Three sheets of paper for each pair of students
■ Scissors
■ Glue
■ Blackline masters of shapes A, B, and C, pages 169–171
■ Blackline master of menu activity, page 168

Getting started

■ Post the samples of shapes A, B, and C. Explain to the students that you cut the designs from the same size paper squares they used to make their rockets. Just as with *Rocket Shapes,* explain that you used one full square for each shape.

■ Give the children a moment to imagine how you cut the squares. Ask them not to tell their ideas at this time but just visualize what they might do to create those shapes.

■ Tell the children that they will be working in pairs. They will have plenty of squares, so if one idea doesn't work, they can throw away all the pieces, get another square, and try a new idea. When they've made a shape, they should paste it onto a sheet of paper, using a separate piece of paper for each shape.

■ Explain that after making all three shapes, each child should choose a shape and write about how he or she cut the square and arranged the pieces. Encourage students to confer with their partners to be sure that someone else could follow their directions and make the same shape.

■ When the children have completed this activity, bring them together to share their results. Have some describe how they made their designs. Invite a few children to read what they wrote and discuss how the information they included helps the listener understand the directions. Ask the children to imagine how they might return each shape to the original square.

FROM THE CLASSROOM

I posted the three shapes I had prepared and said, "I made these shapes from the same size squares that you used to make your rockets."

"All right!" "Neat!" the children responded.

"I cut my paper square into four pieces to make this shape," I said, pointing to shape A. "I used the whole square, and I didn't throw any pieces away." I was interested in having the children try to visualize what I might have done. "Can you imagine how you might do that?" I asked.

Stacy asked, "Did you use only one paper?" I nodded and she said, "Really?" Other children were also looking in amazement. The length of my paper square compared with the greater length of shape A seemed to challenge the children's perceptions.

Raul raised his hand. "I know how to do B," he said.

"You'll get a chance to try," I said, "because in this activity, you and a partner will use a square to make each of the three shapes I posted."

I showed them the pile of squares. "You might have to try several times before you find out how to cut the square and put the pieces together into each shape," I said. "That's fine. It's not expensive paper. Just be sure to throw away all the pieces from the last try before you start over."

I gave one more direction. "After you've made all three shapes, each of you should choose one shape to write about. When you write, explain how you cut the paper to get the pieces you used. What did you do first, second, and then third? I'd like you to write so clearly that I could follow your directions and do it myself."

Observing the Children

Before most of the children had settled into their work, Elena was already carefully using a ruler to draw the diagonals on a square. "I saw it right away," she told me, pointing to design A.

"Is this okay?" Gabriel asked me. He was also working on design A. Gabriel showed me the four little triangles he had snipped from the corners of his square.

"No," I said, "you need to make your triangles the same size and shape as in the example."

Gabriel and his partner, Stacy, threw their scraps away and got new squares. They tried the same strategy, this time snipping off larger triangles. "It's not right, is it?" said Stacy.

I could see the beginnings of frustration, so I took the children up to the sample shapes. Stacy held her square next to shape A. "You mean you made it out of a paper just like this?" she asked incredulously.

"Yes," I answered.

"This one too?" she asked. I nodded yes.

Gabriel was looking at design B. "Wait," he said, "I know how to do that." He used his finger to trace where he would cut the paper.

"Why don't you start with that one?" I suggested, and the two children returned to their seats.

"My partner had to go take a test," Javier announced.

"What are you going to do?" I asked him. As a class, we have discussed three options for students whose partners aren't present: finding someone else without a partner, working alone, or joining another pair and making a group of three. I wanted Javier to decide for himself. He looked around. Raul was also without a partner, and the two went off to get started.

Raul drew a diagram to help explain how he had cut his square.

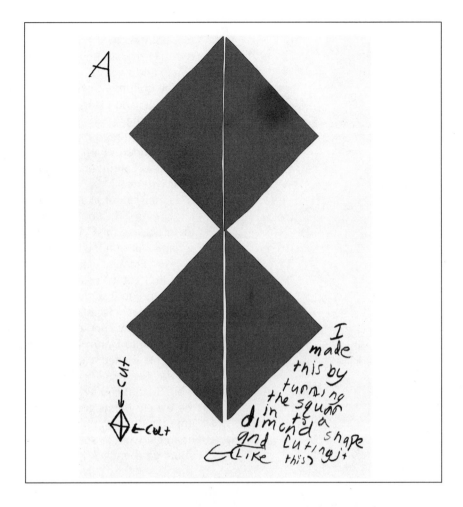

A

↑ cut

←cut

I made this by turning the square into a dimond shape and cuting it (like this)

Raquel and Linda were partners. Linda was gluing pieces to make shape A. "How'd she do that?" I heard Raquel murmur. But before long, I saw her explaining to Linda where the triangles for shape C came from.

Adrian and Elena were deep in discussion. Elena had finished shape C. "How much paper did you use?" asked Adrian. Elena assured him that she'd used only one square, and she leaned over to explain that she'd cut off the corners of the square to get the triangles.

A big smile spread over Adrian's face. "Oh, I get it!" he said.

Martha got my attention as I walked by. "Will you help me with this one?" she asked. Martha was referring to shape B, the one that was fairly easy for most of the children. I sat down next to her.

"What are you thinking of doing?" I asked. I wanted to see how she approached the problem. Martha showed me how she had folded her paper twice to get four equal squares. "Do you think that will work?" I asked her.

"I think so," she said, beginning to cut.

I moved on to Jonathan. He was also folding his paper, working on shape A. "What are you trying?" I asked him.

Jonathan explained his idea. "I folded it in a triangle and then I folded it into another triangle."

I returned to Linda and Raquel. "We did it different ways," the girls told me, pointing to shape A. Raquel had drawn an "X" on her paper from corner to corner and cut on the line. Linda said, "I didn't. I folded it once, twice, and I got it!"

The children chattered as they worked. I watched them try different strategies, and I stopped now and then to ask them what they were thinking or doing.

When children moved to the writing phase, my role shifted. When individual students came to me to share what they wrote, I listened to them read aloud and then I gave feedback. I continually pushed for clarity in their writing.

Francisca, for example, wrote about shape B: *I cut out just four squares.*

"Hmmm," I said. "I'm not sure I understand. You mean you just cut them out like this?" I picked up a newsprint square and arbitrarily cut four squares out of it. "Is this what you mean?" I asked.

"No," Francisca laughed. "I folded it in the middle and then folded it again."

"Oh, I get it," I said. I folded the paper as she directed and then opened it. "Then you just glued it flat on your paper like this, right?"

"No," Francisca laughed again. "I had to cut it first."

I encouraged her to write all that she had explained to me, and off she went.

I spoke to Danny about his paragraph, which he was writing haphazardly. He looked away, and told me about his great-uncle who had died the day before. "They're going to sing to him," Danny told me. We talked a bit. School is only one facet of children's lives. I respected the fact that there were things going on in Danny's life that right now were more important to him than geometry. Then I gave Danny a few options for how he might want to spend the rest of math time. "You might draw or write about your uncle," I said, "or revisit a menu item you've already done."

I asked Alma to add another sentence to explain how she had cut her paper into four squares.

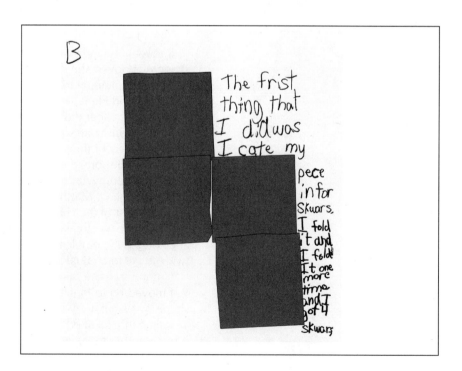

A few children really struggled to put their thoughts into writing. Adrian was one of them. I waited until he'd had a chance to begin writing to the best of his ability. Then I offered to take dictation. Sometimes other children help Adrian in this way.

A few other children in the class were just beginning to write, and much of their spelling was invented. I often had trouble understanding their papers when I read them later. To avoid this problem, I asked students to read their papers to me. I jotted down the unclear words on a Post-It™ Note and affixed it to the child's paper at a later time.

After a little encouragement, Francisca explained how she made shape B.

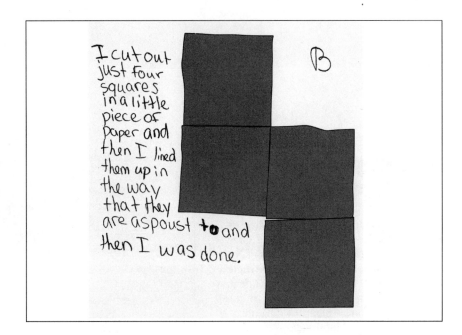

I cut out just four squares in a little piece of paper and then I lined them up in the way that they are aspoust to and then I was done.

A Class Discussion

The children gathered on the rug, their papers in hand. I planned to have some children read their writing and ask others to comment on the parts that helped them understand the writer's methods.

"Were any of the shapes easier than others?" I asked.

"A was cinchy," Francisca said. When Steve disagreed, she allowed, "Well, I had trouble with C."

"How did you make shape A?" I inquired. "Would you like to read what you wrote?"

Francisca read from her paper. *I just cut out four triangles and then I put them together two of them and then we paste them together and then I made them touch then I was done.*

I asked the class, "What did Francisca write that helped you understand how she made the shape?"

"She did it with four triangles," said Raul.

"And they had to touch," added Jonathan.

I encouraged the class to consider how to communicate clearly. "Is there anything else you would like to know?" I asked.

Danny raised his hand. "What about the other triangles? You said two."

"Then I put two more together," Francisca told him.

I thanked Francisca for sharing and asked the children to look at shape A and imagine what they would have to do to put the triangles back into a square. I paused for a moment to give the children an opportunity to visualize how the triangles might fit together again.

"What would you have to do to the triangles?" I then asked. Elena had an answer. "The triangles have to turn to make an X again."

"Who would like to share how to make another shape?" I asked the class. Stacy took a paper square to show us how she had made shape C.

Making this design reminded Stacy of folding paper airplanes.

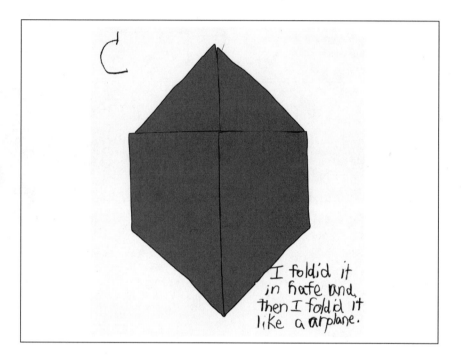

C

I foldid it
in hafe and,
then I foldid it
like a arplane.

She drew lines indicating her first cuts. "I did this," she said, "and then this," drawing a third line up the middle. "I needed to move the triangles here," she said, pointing to the bottom of the square.

Stacy read her explanation: *I foldid it in hafe and then I foldid it like a arplane.* I asked the class, "What did Stacy write that helped you understand the way she made shape C?"

"I really knew what she said," Danny told us. "I did it that way too."

"Can anyone see how to rearrange shape C to change it back to a square?" I asked. The children were silent.

"That's hard," Steve said.

"Oooh, I know," Alma said. "Those triangles on top just have to go to the bottom. See?" Alma was excited about her discovery.

"I don't get it," Gabriel complained.

"Oh, I see," Steve said. Visualizing is easier for some children than for others.

I could tell from the wiggling that many children were ready for recess. I decided to continue at another time.

Martha described how she made shape C.

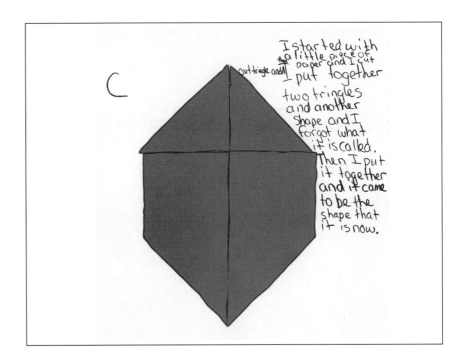

C

I started with a little piece of paper and I cut the out tringle and I put together two tringles and another shape and I forgot what it is called. Then I put it together and it came to be the shape that it is now.

Gabriel wrote: *Square Designs. I cut a diamond out of a square. First I folded the square on the diagonal. They came out in the shape of triangles.*

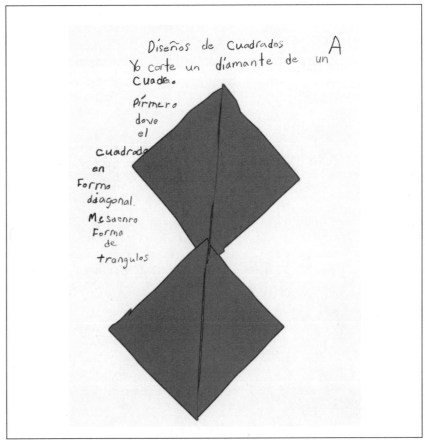

Diseños de Cuadrados   A
Yo corte un diamante de un cuado.

Pirmero dove el cuadrado en forma diagonal.
Me saenro forma de trangulos

MENU ACTIVITY

Cloak Patterns

Overview

This activity is an extension of the whole class lesson *A Cloak for the Dreamer.* (See page 42.) Each pair of students makes a second cloak for the Archduke, this time using two different shapes to create the pattern. A class discussion focuses the children on the shapes within each of the cloak designs.

172

Cloak Patterns

You need: Two different tagboard shapes
(square, rectangle, or triangle)
Construction paper (two colors)
12-by-18-inch newsprint
Glue
Scissors

1. Choose two shapes and two colors of construction paper. Using both colors, trace and cut out four to eight pieces of each shape. You can cut shapes in whatever color combinations you like.

2. Arrange all the shapes so that the sides match and the pattern pleases you. When you have a design you like, glue it onto a sheet of newsprint.

From *Math By All Means: Geometry, Grade 2*   ©1994 Math Solutions Publications

Before the lesson

Gather the same materials used to make the first cloak in the whole class lesson *A Cloak for the Dreamer:*

▪ Tagboard shapes for tracing (Transfer patterns on page 173 to tagboard, making four or five of each shape.)
▪ Construction paper in different colors
▪ One sheet of 12-by-18-inch newsprint for each pair of children
▪ Scissors
▪ Glue
▪ The children's designs from the whole class lesson *A Cloak for the Dreamer*
▪ Blackline master of menu activity, page 172

Getting started

▪ Show some of the children's patterns from the whole class lesson *A Cloak for the Dreamer.* To reinforce the correct procedure for making cloak patterns, choose only those designs with same-length sides matching and without gaps or overlaps. Have the children explain the problem with a cloak made of circles and why their cloak designs are better.

▪ Explain to the children that they will make a second cloak pattern, this time using two different shapes. Tell the children that they will again use two colors of construction paper, and that they need to cut out from four to eight of each shape–in whatever combination of two colors they want.

▪ Encourage the children to explore different shape arrangements before choosing one to glue down. If they like, the children may cut additional shapes to complete their design.

▪ When children finish their patterns, start a class discussion. How can they describe the patterns? What shapes do they notice? (Use the Geometry Words chart as a reference for terminology.) How are the designs the same? How are they different?

FROM THE CLASSROOM

I held up Stacy and Linda's cloak pattern from the whole class lesson.

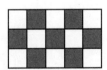

"I see a pattern!" said Gabriel. "It goes red, purple, red, purple, red, purple."
"Can anyone describe the pattern in a different way?" I inquired.
Adrian had an idea. "Red, purple, red. Purple, red, purple. Red, purple, red." He was reading the pattern vertically.
"It's like a checkerboard," Linda added.
I next showed Javier and Alejandra's pattern. They had used purple and pink rectangles. "Let's see the different ways you can describe this pattern," I said.

"A maze, it's a maze," Martha commented.

"Look," said Danny, and he traced a pink path that wandered from one side of the paper to the other.

"Tell us about your design," I urged Javier and Alejandra.

Alejandra showed us how they had laid the rectangles along the bottom of the paper, then up the side, then along the top, spiraling around the paper's edge, until it was completely filled in. And all the while they had alternated colors.

Alejandra and Javier's intricate pattern suddenly became clear to me. I mused about how we, teacher and students, had exchanged roles. So often it is the teacher who sees a pattern or concept clearly and is trying to help the child become aware of it. In this case, Alejandra had helped me see a pattern that was obvious to her.

After discussing a few more of the children's patterns, I asked, "Do you think these cloaks would keep the Archduke warm and dry? Do they have any gaps?"

The children agreed that the cloaks would work well. "There are some little spaces," explained Stacy, "because it's hard to cut exactly right."

I went on to introduce the new activity. "You and your partner are going to make another cloak for the Archduke. Again you'll use two different colors. Your shapes need to fit right up against one another, and they can't overlap.

"But your cloak will be different in one way," I continued. "This time your cloak is going to have two different shapes in it." I held up the tagboard shapes. "You can pick any two of these shapes, and you'll need to cut from four to eight of each. You might want six large rectangles and six small squares. Or eight large triangles and five small triangles. You decide on how many of each shape and what colors to use."

"Do a little experimenting with the shapes before you glue them down," I added, "and find a design you like the best. Try to make this cloak a very special one." Then I added, "If you need to cut out a few more shapes to complete your design, and you have time, that's fine."

Adrian and Steve put two triangles together to make squares.

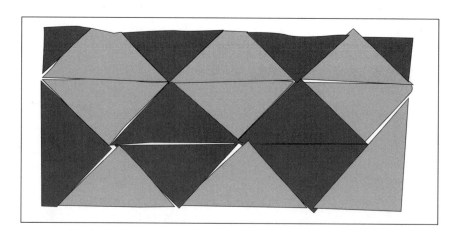

Observing the Children

The children were busy gathering their materials. Most had chosen to do this activity. I find that when I introduce a new activity, it usually attracts many children's interest.

Elena and Alma had no problem choosing shapes. "Let's each pick one," suggested Alma. Elena selected the large triangle and Elena the small rectangle, and they left to search for scissors.

I walked over to Martha and Danny, who were tracing large squares and triangles. Martha had placed the square right in the middle of a sheet of construction paper, and began to cut from the edge.

"You're wasting paper," Danny observed. "You should cut it at the corner."

Stacy was behind me, construction paper in hand. "Look, it's a little duck!" she laughed, showing me the irregular shape that was left.

Raul and Francisca were working together, Raul cutting out red large squares and Francisca tracing and cutting small yellow ones.

Alma and Elena had cut out six large triangles and eight small rectangles. Elena was laying the rectangles along the long side of the triangle and found that they didn't fit. "Do they have to match?" she asked. I nodded. Elena turned the rectangles and tried the same procedure, finding that once again the shapes didn't match.

Alma reached over to get a triangle and some rectangles. She laid the shapes against one another in different ways.

I moved on to Marcos and Gabriel, who were working well together. They tried an arrangement for their large squares and triangles, grouping the yellow shapes together and the black shapes together. "It looks like a shoe," commented Marcos. "Let's try a new one."

Before Marcos could remove the shapes from the paper, Gabriel said excitedly, "I've got an idea!" He moved a few shapes and cut a square into two triangles. "Look! It's a black bat!"

Stacy and Linda had chosen triangles and rectangles and were fitting them together in different ways. "Look, a square," said Stacy, as she placed two triangles together, long sides touching. "Can we make a checkerboard?" she wondered aloud. Later I found that the girls had indeed made a checkerboard by combining the rectangles together to make more squares.

Francisca and Raul were trying to decide what to do with the two little squares that stuck out from the rectangular cloak they had made. "I know," Raul finally decided. "That's for the Archduke's neck. He can tie it there."

A Class Discussion

The children sat with their partners, cloak designs in hand, waiting to share with the class.

Linda and Stacy got up in front of the class to show their design made of triangles and rectangles. "We made another checkerboard," Stacy told the class. It did look like their other design; they had used different colors and had combined the shapes to make another checkerboard pattern. "It goes blue, orange, blue, orange," Linda explained.

"It's got holes," said Danny. "I can see the white between." He was right, but it seemed as if the spaces were due to lack of coordination with scissors.

"You know," I said, "it looks to me as if they did their best. I think the Archduke will be just fine in that cloak."

NOTE Inviting some children to show their cloak patterns has three benefits. Those who share have the chance to verbalize their geometric thinking. Students who observe see a variety of approaches to the activity. And the teacher can reiterate the directions as well as help children understand the kinds of results that are acceptable.

Linda and Stacy discovered how to make a
checkerboard with triangles and rectangles.

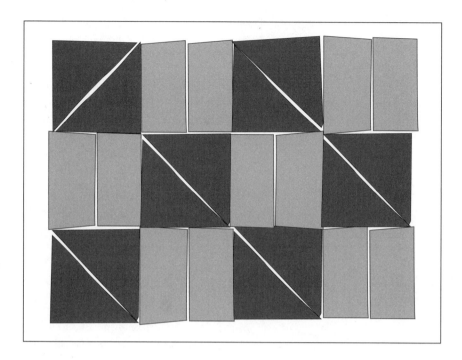

Marcos and Gabriel got up to share their design. "It's Batman," Gabriel
explained proudly.

I pointed to the body of the bat. "How would you describe that shape?"
I asked.

"It's got four sides," said Gabriel.

"And four corners," added Marcos.

"What you described sounds like a square to me," I said. "Is that a square?"

"No," said Francisca, "but it still has four sides. They're just longer on
the bottom and shorter on the top."

"What is the math name for this shape?" I asked.

"There it is," said Alejandra, jumping up to point to the Geometry Words
chart. "Trapezoid," she read. I asked the students to say the word together.

"See if you and your partner can find the shapes that Marcos and
Gabriel put together to make the trapezoid," I said. After a moment, hands
went up and I called on Adrian. "It's a square and two rectangles—I mean
triangles," he corrected himself.

"Does anyone see another shape in this design?" I asked.

"I see a hexagon," said Francisca. She seemed proud to use that word.

"How do you know it's a hexagon?" I asked her.

"Six sides," she said breezily.

Martha and Danny volunteered to share their design. "It's a hawk or a
vulture," he said, always eager to think in pictures. Danny showed us the
wings and the beak. Other children saw Danny's bird and built on his
ideas. Javier decided it was an owl and pointed out the ruff around its
neck. On and on the children talked, about the hourglass they saw or the
face they imagined.

The children saw a hawk, an owl, and an hourglass in Martha and Danny's design.

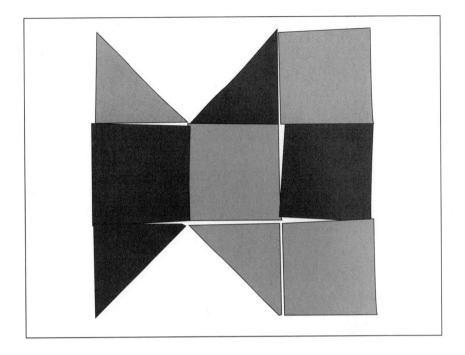

The children did not share all their cloaks the same day. Other children got to share when empty moments appeared—at the beginning or end of math time or at other times during the school day. The discussions were rich, spanning many aspects of the designs. The children enjoyed the beauty of the patterns. They talked about the shapes they saw, and how shapes were the same or different. The children noticed the new shapes created by smaller shapes placed side by side. And they talked about the images they saw, relating the shapes to things they knew in their own worlds.

MENU ACTIVITY

More Shapes on the Geoboard

Overview

This activity extends the whole class lesson *Triangles on the Geoboard* (see page 49) but focuses on properties of regular and irregular polygons. The children work individually to create shapes on the geoboard and copy them onto geoboard dot paper. The class then sorts and classifies the shapes in several ways.

174

More Shapes on the Geoboard I

You need: One geoboard
         One rubber band
         Dot paper
         Scissors
         Tape or thumbtacks for posting

1. Make several different shapes on the geoboard. Each shape must follow these rules:
   - It must be made with one rubber band.
   - The rubber band must not cross over itself.
   - The shape must stay in one piece when you cut it out.

2. Choose one of your shapes. Make sure that it's different from those already posted.

3. Copy the shape onto dot paper and cut it out. Write your name on the back and post it.

From *Math By All Means: Geometry, Grade 2* ©1994 Math Solutions Publications

Before the lesson

Gather these materials:
- ■ Geoboards and rubber bands
- ■ Geoboard dot paper (See the Blackline Masters section, page 175.)
- ■ Scissors
- ■ Rulers
- ■ Tape or thumbtacks (for posting shapes)
- ■ Blackline master of menu activity, page 174

Getting started

■ Introduce the activity. Tell the children they will work as they did for *Triangles on the Geoboard*, with two differences. First, they will work by themselves. Second, they can create shapes other than triangles.

■ Read the rules for making the shapes.

■ Clarify the rules by showing the class the following examples on a geoboard. After each example, ask if the shape follows the rule and have the children explain why.

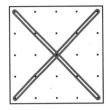

(No, because it uses more than one rubber band and they cross over.)

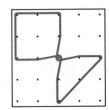

(No, because the shape would be in two pieces when you cut it out.)

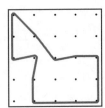

(This shape is okay.)

■ Ask students to experiment making many different shapes and then to choose one. Tell them to copy the shape onto dot paper, cut it out, write their name on the back, and post it. Show them where you'd like the shapes posted. Tell the children that their shape must be different from the shapes already posted.

■ After several days, when all the children have posted their shapes, choose a place for sorting the shapes. You may wish to sort them on the board or place a large sheet of butcher paper on the rug with the children gathered around.

■ Ask the students to look at the shapes and talk about which ones belong together or are the same in some way. For example, a child might say, "These two go together because they both are short." Ask if any other shapes fit into that group, then arrange the shapes into two sets: those that are short, those that are not short. You may want to arrange the shapes into a graph, placing the shapes into two rows.

■ Rearrange the shapes so that they are no longer sorted into two groups. Ask if anyone sees another way the shapes can be sorted. A child might say, "Those shapes have five sides." Sort the shapes into two new sets, those that have five sides and those that do not. Take advantage of opportunities to use mathematical language, such as the names for shapes ("pentagons" in this case) and words for the relative sizes of shapes (smaller, shortest, wider).

■ If time and interest allow, have children identify a third way to sort the shapes. If not, collect the shapes and plan to continue sorting at a later time.

■ After students have had experience with this activity do the *Describing Shapes* assessment. (See page 110.)

FROM THE CLASSROOM

I showed the children the menu instructions and read the title. "You've already explored triangles on the geoboard," I said. "For this menu activity, you can explore other shapes on the geoboard."

I pointed to the "I" in the upper right corner of the task. "What does this 'I' mean?" I asked the children.

"Individual," said Carmen.

"You don't need a partner," Adrian explained.

Next, the children and I read aloud the list of materials each child would need: a geoboard, a rubber band, dot paper, scissors, tape or thumbtacks.

"It's the same thing we already did," Danny observed.

"It's a similar activity," I acknowledged, "but this time we'll be exploring lots of different shapes, not just triangles."

I continued by reading the instructions: *Make several different shapes on the geoboard. Each shape must follow these rules: It must be made with one rubber band. The rubber band must not cross over itself. The shape must stay in one piece when you cut it out.*

I showed the children a few examples on my geoboard. "Is this shape okay?" I asked, holding up a shape that did not follow the rule.

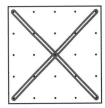

Many heads were shaking no. "Why not?" I asked.
"Because," explained Raul, "the rubber band makes an X."
"Who can explain it in a different way?" I asked.
"It can't be overlapped," Jonathan contributed.
"How about this shape?" I asked, showing a shape that did follow the rule.

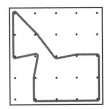

"It's okay," said Elena, "because you could cut it out."
I made another shape. "Is this one okay?" I asked.

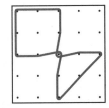

"No," said Alejandra, "they're two shapes already. One's like a square and one's like a triangle. It would fall apart."

I continued, "After you've explored a lot of shapes, then follow the remaining instructions: *Choose one of your shapes. Make sure that it's different from those already posted. Copy the shape onto dot paper and cut it out. Write your name on the back and post it.*" The children would be using their own shapes for a written assessment later, so it was necessary for them to write their names on their shapes.

I gave a last reminder before having the children begin their menu work. "Remember that the shape that you post has to be one that no one else has posted yet. It must be different from all the others," I told the children. "If you notice that your shape matches one that is already posted, then make a new one." then then make a new onethen make a new one."

Observing the Children

About half the class chose to work on the new activity. Javier began to copy the first shape he made. I encouraged him to make several different shapes before deciding on one to transfer to the dot paper.

Jonathan sat down with his materials. "I like these," he announced to no one in particular. I watched him make an "L" shape, an irregular hexagon, and then a shape somewhat like a "J." "'J' for 'Jonathan,'" he told me. Jonathan chose to copy his next shape, a trapezoid, and did so quickly and efficiently.

Raquel was working in a leisurely manner. I watched as she made an assortment of pentagons and quadrilaterals. Raquel looked up at me. "Look, I made a fat one!" she said.

"That certainly is a fat pentagon," I answered, supplying the terminology for her.

Alma showed me her geoboard. "Look," she said, "I made the Pizza Hut sign."

"That's a hexagon," I told her.

Alma looked at me in surprise. "I didn't know that," she said. "It's not like the yellow block." We fished out a yellow hexagon from the Pattern Blocks and compared it to Alma's hexagon. Alma counted the sides. "They both have six," she announced.

I watched the explorations in progress. Raul was helping Steve copy the same 10-sided shape that was on his own board.

I noticed Gabriel spinning his geoboard by one of the pegs. I reminded him that he needed to use the materials sensibly. "Why do you think you shouldn't twirl the geoboard?" I asked him.

"It could break," Gabriel answered, looking down.

"That's right," I responded. "I'll be watching to see you use the geoboard carefully." I moved on, wondering whether I should have reviewed how we use the geoboard when I gave the instructions.

I noticed that Elena had created an intricate 13-sided figure. She began to copy it onto a piece of paper.

Alejandra struggled as she tried to copy a rectangle. She looked up at me. "Did it come out right?" she asked.

"What do you think?" I answered.

"No . . . " she said uncertainly as she considered both her drawing and geoboard. Then she counted the pegs along one side of the rectangle. "No, I want to change it," she said. She erased one side and extended two other sides. Content, she went off to get the tape.

I noticed that Gabriel seemed to like a seven-sided figure he had made. "It looks like a bird," he smiled.

I watched as Adrian began to copy his shape. He was biting his lip, his hand gripping the pencil hard, stopping to erase from time to time. In comparison, Elena easily traced her intricate shape.

Martha brought me the triangle that she had copied onto dot paper. The sides were not at all straight. I knew that Martha could do better. I asked her to do it again and try to draw the sides as straight as they were on the geoboard. "Try using a ruler," I suggested.

I noticed that Raquel had made a shape on her geoboard but had not yet begun copying it. "I see you've made a hexagon," I told her. "Now what are you going to do?" Raquel went to get dot paper.

I watched Javier, deep in concentration, as he copied his eight-sided "sword" onto the dot paper. He worked slowly but accurately, counting the dots as he went.

NOTE It's important for students to learn to use manipulative materials appropriately. From time to time, you may need to discuss the use of a material with a child or with the entire class.

A Class Discussion

When all the children had completed this menu task, I gathered them on the rug to examine the shapes and sort them by different characteristics. To provide an area for sorting, I laid a large sheet of butcher paper on the rug and placed all the shapes on it. The children sat in a circle around the paper.

"How did we do?" I asked the children. "Are all our shapes different?"

The children looked at the shapes. Adrian was smiling. "That's mine!" he said, showing a sense of ownership in the activity.

The children decided that all the shapes were indeed different. I continued, "I'd like to organize the shapes in some way. I'll give you a moment to think about shapes that could go together."

Danny had an idea. "This is two, that is three," he said.

I was confused. "Two and three what?" I asked.

"Three sides," Danny said.

I still didn't understand what he was saying. "Show us," I suggested.

Danny counted the dots on the sides of the shapes and sorted the shapes into two groups, those that had a side with three dots and those that did not. Now I understood what he was doing. I'm glad to have these periodic chances to be confused by a student's idea. It reminds me that children must sometimes feel the same way when teachers give explanations.

I saw an opportunity to add to the students' terminology. I picked up a shape. "Which side has three dots?" I asked. The children showed me.

"Let's turn it so that the side with the three dots is the base," I said. I rotated the shape so the side they identified was on the bottom. We continued rotating and laying the shapes against the bottom of the butcher paper. The children helped me place the shapes with three-dot bases in one group. Those without a three-dot side went into a different group.

"I know another way," said Francisca. The class watched as she sorted the shapes into two groups. "These all have one dot inside and these don't," she explained.

"What about this one?" asked Stacy. "It's got three dots." Francisca moved that shape to the other group.

"Does anyone have any other way to sort our shapes?" I asked.

Raul had an idea. "Some have an X shape," he said. Raul put several shapes together, some that clearly had an X shape and some that were less obvious but did qualify.

Raul put these two shapes together because they "have an X shape."

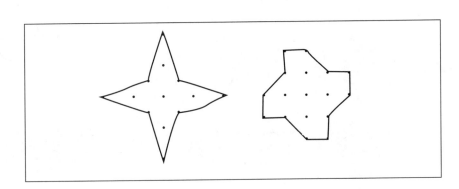

Danny took exception to one of Raul's decisions. "What's he going to do with that?" Danny demanded.

I intervened, saying, "Right now, let him organize the shapes in his own way."

Raul reconsidered the shape, then removed it from the group. "It's not pointy enough," he decided.

We looked at the remaining shapes. "If these all look like the letter X, then what letter could this one be?" I held up a shape.

"A Z," the children said. Raul's letter-shape suggestion seemed to intrigue the children. More ideas tumbled out.

This shape reminded the children of a Z.

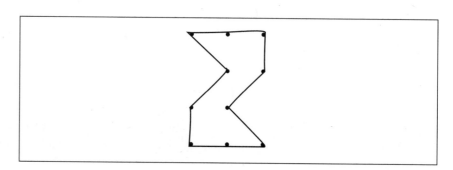

"The square is an O," said Gabriel.

"If this had a dot, it would be an i," Amanda told us, pointing to a long trapezoid.

Stacy had an idea. "Here's one that looks like a V," she said.

"You know," said Linda, "if the X was turned on its side it would be like a t."

The comparisons broadened to things in their world. "This looks like a face with two eyes," said Raul.

Then the same idea came to both Raul and Jonathan. "This one could be a hat!" they chorused.

The children combined shapes made by Raul, Jonathan, Danny, and Francisca to make a person.

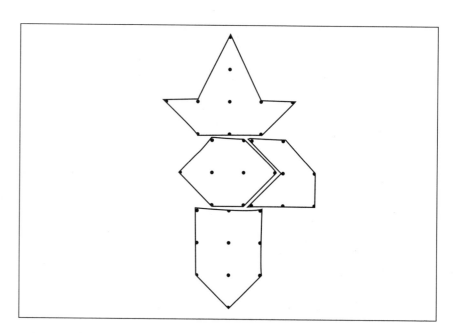

Raul laughed. "Let's put them together," he said, "and it's a face with a hat."

Francisca joined in. "This could be the hair," she said, adding a shape next to the face and the hat.

"And this is the tie," said Danny, putting a pentagon under the face.

I felt that we were ready to move on. "How else can we organize our shapes?" I asked the group.

Danny began to move the shapes around. I urged him to think aloud for us.

"I'm counting the sides," he explained. "These two have 12."

Martha reached over to check. "This has 11," she stated.

"Nuh-uh," countered Javier, "it does so have 12." He and Adrian leaned over to count. "See?"

Children reached over to count the sides on the shapes nearest to them. "This has 5," said Francisca.

"And this one has 6," Amanda told the group.

"Look," said Danny, as he arranged the shapes into a graph, putting the shapes with the same number of sides in separate rows.

"Explain to us what you're doing," I said.

"This line has the highest number of sides," said Danny. "There are 13. And this line has 12 sides, this one has 8, this one has 7, this one has 6, this one has 5, and this one has 4."

Raul disagreed with the placement of a shape, so he reached over to count and check. Danny was right.

I asked a question to encourage the children to interpret the information on the graph. "What lines have the fewest shapes in it?" I asked. The children agreed they were the lines containing shapes with 13 and 7 sides.

Elena made a 13-sided figure.

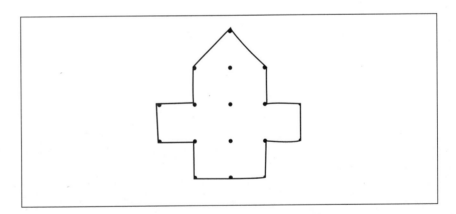

"What else does the graph tell us?" I asked.

"Three shapes have 12 sides," Elena said.

"These two lines are even," Raquel told us, pointing to the lines with pentagons and octagons.

"And lines 4, 6, and 12 have three shapes in them," Amanda said.

I ended the sorting activity here, pleased with the variety of ways the children had looked at their shapes. I taped the shapes onto the butcher paper and posted the graph, so children could continue to examine it.

ASSESSMENT Describing Shapes

In this assessment, children first talk in pairs about the shapes they made for the menu activity *More Shapes on the Geoboard.* (See page 102.) Then they individually write descriptions of their shapes. The students' papers give information about the geometric language they feel comfortable using.

Demonstrate how the children will talk in pairs by having a student volunteer to be your partner. You each choose one of the geoboard dot paper shapes and take turns describing it, each time giving just one characteristic. When you think the activity is clear to the rest of the class, ask students to choose shapes and talk with their partners about them.

After partners have had time to talk about their shapes with one another, stop them and explain the writing assignment. Tell the children they are to write about their shape, describing it in as many ways as they can. Explain that they will work individually so that you can learn about all of their ideas. Tell them that they should include information about what the shape reminds them of, its size, the number of sides and corners it has, and if possible, its name.

"Who would like to be my partner to demonstrate this activity?" I asked. Amanda volunteered.

Amanda and I each selected a shape from the pile of shapes that the children had drawn. Each of us took turns telling something she noticed about her chosen shape.

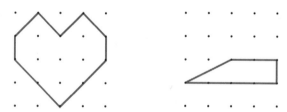

"Mine looks like a heart," Amanda said.

"Mine looks like a shoe," I said.

"My shape has a point down at the bottom," said Amanda.

"Look at this," I said. "My shape looks short and wide now, but if I turn it this way . . . "

" . . . it's skinny," finished Steve.

Amanda whispered as she counted the sides, and then said, "My shape has eight sides. Is it an octagon?"

"It sure is," I said. "Mine has four sides. It's a quadrilateral. This quadrilateral has a special name: It's a 'trapezoid.' Only two of its sides are parallel."

"My shape has six dots inside," contributed Amanda.

I noted, "Mine doesn't have any dots inside it at all. If I turn my shape around, it looks like a pencil."

"Or a rocket!" added the children. Somehow I knew they were going to say that.

I gave the children their directions. "You'll work in pairs. Each of you will choose a shape. You will do the same thing that Amanda and I did—talk about your shape. Take turns to describe your shape as many ways as you can."

There was a flurry of picking partners and choosing shapes. A few minutes later I found myself next to Alma and Linda, who were deep in conversation about their shapes.

Linda said, "This looks like the 'L' in my name." And she traced around it with her pencil.

Alma looked at her own shape and said, "This looks like the things the clowns use." She reached for another way to explain her thought. "Like a barrel," she added.

"Like this?" asked Linda, and she drew a trapezoid on a piece of paper.

"Mmmm, yes," agreed Alma, peering over Linda's arm.

"Mine has five sides," said Linda.

"I can turn mine on the side and it looks like a square," said Alma.

"Let me see," said Linda. She examined the drawing. "Yeah!"

"Or," added Alma, "I put it like this and it looks like a baby's crib."

"Or a tub!" Linda decided.

Explaining the Assignment

I could see that the children were having no problem coming up with things to say about their shapes. I called for the children's attention. "You've been talking a lot about your shapes, and it sounds as if you have a lot to say," I began. "But I'd like to learn all your ideas about your shape, so I want you to write them down now. Please write by yourself, without a partner, so that I can see what each of you knows about your shape. Also, I'd like you to draw your shape on your paper so I know what it looks like."

Children's heads leaned over papers as they quickly began to write down their thoughts. I was amazed at how amenable they were to writing and how much they wrote. Certainly the time spent talking about the topic with a partner had helped.

The murmur of children sounding out words and consulting with one another spread throughout the room. I heard Steve ask Jonathan, "How do you spell 'with'?"

Adrian's paper was blank except for his name and a drawing of his polygon and a few letters. Writing was still very difficult for him. I volunteered to take dictation.

The Children's Responses

As I reviewed each child's work, I looked for several things. First, did the child relate the shape to something in the real world? If so, the child was perceiving the characteristics of the shape as a whole and identifying an object that had those same characteristics.

For example, Carmen made these comparisons: *Es como un cojon tien cuatro escinas parese un papalote Parese un cojon de una momia* [It's like a box that has four sides. It looks like a kite. It looks like a mummy box.]

NOTE Writing about mathematics is always easier for children when they've first had the opportunity to express their ideas orally. Having children talk in pairs is a helpful way to prepare them for putting their ideas on paper.

Javier showed his understanding of the shape as a whole by comparing it to a volcano and a pyramid.

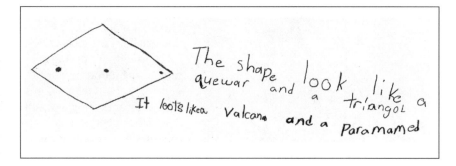

Martha explained what her shape would look like if it were rotated: *My shape lookes like a Z and a two . . . If you trnit a rond it will look like a N.*

Martha compared her shape to a "Z" and a "2." She described some features of her shape, then explained how the shape would look if it were rotated.

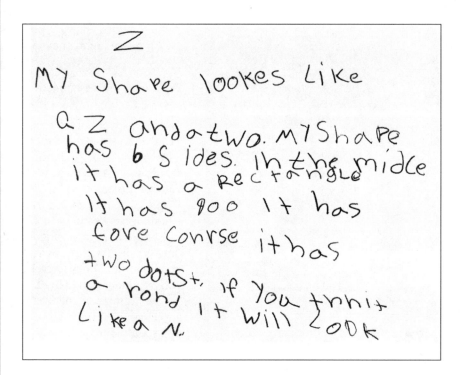

Many children went further in their descriptions. I noted whether they examined the specific features of the shape. Did the child talk about the components of the shape: its angles, its corners, its sides? Did he note how many angles, how many corners, how many sides? Did she talk about the relative width or length of those components? A child who can discuss these features is beginning to analyze the properties that differentiate one shape from another.

Steve was starting to notice these features. He wrote: *To me it looks like a bed and a house. And it has six cornes and it has five sides. And if you turn it up side down it looks like a bed whit one foot.*

I found that some children's papers indicated that they were exceptionally flexible in how they looked at their shapes. They identified smaller shapes within their larger shapes. Some children even described what might happen if other shapes were added to their shape. They predicted what would happen when shapes were combined or divided.

For example, Francisca wrote: *This shape is like a x. In the midle it has a rectangle It has 13 sides. It has the body of a little stick man. All of the angles are less than 90. It looks like the shape is like the singn of the multipication singn. 15 dots conected.*

Alma compared her shape to objects in the world and flipped the shape to make new comparisons: *Mine looks like a bath tob and flip it over and it looks like a cribe and you keep it strat and it looks like a barow [barrel] that the clows [clowns] weus [use] and flip it over and it looks like a squear and you can make it like a circlore [circle] and a u and filp it over and it look like a pitcher frame and it looks like a trapazit but the one on the paper is biger and this one is smiller.*

Alma compared her shape to many things in the world, mentally flipping the shape to make new comparisons. At the end, she attempted the word "trapezoid" *(trapazit)*.

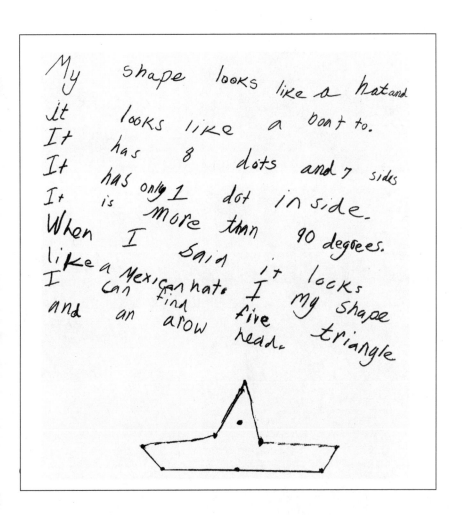

Raul described his shape: *my shape has 13 sides and it has 17 dots it looks like a small soward. It has two small squares on the side and it has a Rectangle on the botom*

Lastly, I was interested in looking at how the children expressed them-selves. What forms of language did they prefer to use? Many children used the language of comparison, such as "It's like a . . . ," "more than," and "skinnier." Some children used the specific terminology we introduced, such as "hexagon."

Alejandra wrote: *mi forma es como un cuadrado. tambien se pueden hacer triangulos. mi forma mide 3 hi medios puntos. mi forma tiene 5 lados y le disen pentagon.* (My shape is like a square. Also you can make triangles. My shape measures 3½ dots. My shape has 5 sides and they call it a pentagon.)

Adrian dictated: *It looks like a shoe. It has 6 dots on the sides. It looks like a shoe but someone took a chunk out of it. It has 6 sides. It's a hexagon.*

Antonio looked at his shape and saw a boat and a Mexican hat. He said that the shape had six sides instead of the actual seven. He used the term "bottom" and explained that bottom meant "on the basement."

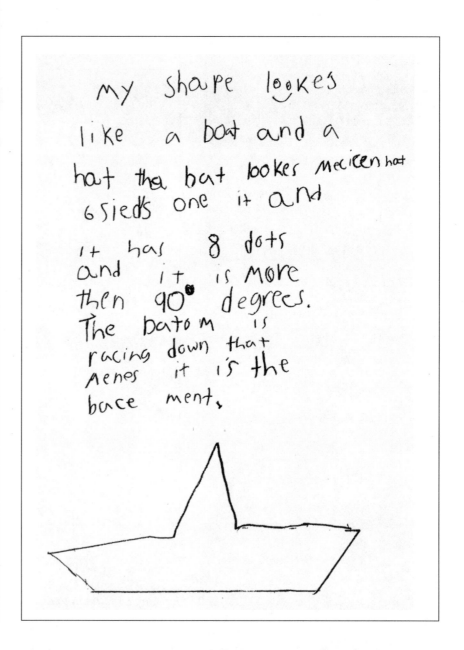

Amanda compared her shape to things in the world, described components of the shape, and identified smaller shapes inside it.

mine looks like a bath tob and flip it over and it looks like a cribe and you keep it strat and it looks like a barow that the clows weus and flip it over and it looks like a squear and you can make it like a circbre and a u and filp it over and it look like a pitcher frame and it looks like a trapazit but the one

on the paper is biger and this one is smiller.

MENU ACTIVITY

Shapes with Six Green Triangles

Overview

This activity is an extension of the whole class lesson *Shapes with Pattern Block Triangles*. (See page 59.) The children arrange six Pattern Block triangles in as many different shapes as possible, making sure that the sides of the triangles match completely. Using triangle paper, the children draw the shapes they make, cut them out, and glue them onto a sheet of colored copier paper. They then write about the shapes they found.

176

Shapes with Six Green Triangles P

You need: 12 green Pattern Block triangles
　　　　　Triangle paper
　　　　　Scissors
　　　　　Glue
　　　　　One sheet of colored paper

1. Using the rule that sides that touch must match completely, make as many different shapes as you can with six triangles.

2. Draw each shape you find on triangle paper and cut it out.

3. Test to make sure each shape is different by trying to match it to each other shape. (Flip, rotate, and turn it to find out.)

4. Glue all the different shapes you find onto a sheet of colored paper.

5. Write about the shapes you found.

From *Math By All Means: Geometry, Grade 2* ©1994 Math Solutions Publications

---

Before the lesson

Gather these materials:
■ 12 green Pattern Block triangles for each pair of students
■ Triangle paper (See Blackline Masters section, page 177.)
■ One sheet of colored copier paper for each pair of students (in a different color from the triangle paper)
■ Glue
■ Scissors
■ Blackline master of menu activity, page 176

Getting started

■ Ask the children to recall the rule they learned for putting triangles together in the *Shapes with Pattern Block Triangles* lesson. Invite a child to use two triangles to demonstrate the rule for the class.

■ Explain that for this menu activity the children work in pairs to find different shapes that can be made with six triangles. Remind the class that if a shape can match another by rotating or flipping, then the two shapes are congruent and don't count as different. Ask the children to predict how many different shapes they think are possible.

■ Tell the students to draw each shape on triangle paper, cut it out, and glue it onto a sheet of colored paper. Remind them to check that each shape is different from those already glued. When they think they've found all of the different shapes, they should write about what shapes they found. Then they should post the sheet for a class discussion.

■ When all the students' sheets are posted, have the class talk about and name the different shapes posted.

Note: There are 12 possible shapes. Do not reveal this to the students. The goal of the activity isn't for students to find all the shapes but to experiment with different arrangements and compare them to be sure they're different. The shapes possible are:

FROM THE CLASSROOM

I reminded the children of the *Shapes with Pattern Block Triangles* activity they had done the previous week. Then I held up two triangles.

"Do you remember the rule about how to put the triangles together?" I asked.

"Sides touching," agreed several children.

"All the way," added Alejandra.

"That's right," I said. To make sure the children remembered the rule, I asked for a volunteer to hold up two triangles and show the ways that the blocks could and could not go together. Raquel demonstrated for the others.

"Last week," I continued, "you investigated all the different shapes that were possible for four and five triangles. This menu activity has you do the same investigation for six triangles. How many different shapes do you think are possible with six triangles?"

"A lot!" Elena said. Others nodded their agreement.

"What is 'a lot'? How many different shapes would you predict?" I asked.

"Maybe ten," said Gabriel, "because we got four shapes with five triangles and you could do a lot with another triangle."

"Six ways," said Steve, "because there are six triangles."

"We'll see what you find out," I said. "Just as you did last time, use the triangle paper to cut out the shapes you make and check to make sure they're different. Then glue the shapes to a piece of paper. When you're finished, write about the shapes you found."

Observing the Children

I watched the children decide which menu items to work on. Martha and Javier got out geoboards to continue *More Shapes on the Geoboard*, as did Stacy and Linda. However, as often happens when I introduce a new menu item, most of the children decided to try it.

Steve and Raul were sitting next to each other, arms crossed, doing nothing as far as I could see. I went over to their table.

"What have you decided to do?" I asked them.

Steve glared at Raul, then begrudgingly said, "The triangle one."

"How many triangles will you be exploring this time?" I asked them.

When Steve said he didn't know, I encouraged him to look at the instruction sheet. The two children counted out six triangles each. Steve made a shape. Raul glanced at Steve's shape and made the same one.

Steve burst out, "He copied me!" There was clearly some problem between the two.

"It's not copying," I explained. "You and your partner should work together to find all the possible shapes. Do you think you and Raul can work together right now, or would you rather work apart for awhile?" If the boys needed some time apart, perhaps they could work individually to find some shapes, and I could help them combine their work later.

Somehow, just having the option to switch seemed to relieve the tension. "We can do it," said Steve, and the boys reached for the materials and began putting the triangles together in different ways.

"I made a duck!" commented Raul.

"Look what I made—a little sled!" said Steve. "If I could get another triangle, I could do a boat."

The boys were exploring but not yet recording. I decided to let them continue and come back in a few minutes to check that they were recording their shapes. I moved on to another table.

Antonio and Josie seemed to be working together effectively. They each made a shape, then checked to see if they had already cut it out. They conferred with each other from time to time.

"Is this the same?" Antonio asked Josie.

Josie reached over and took the shape Antonio had cut out of triangle paper. She flipped it over and placed it on another cut-out shape. "Look," she said, "it is."

Raquel had elected to work alone because her partner was absent. I saw that she had built and was cutting out a shape that did not follow the rule. I chose to intervene. I put two Pattern Block triangles together, sides touching completely. "Does this shape follow the rule?" I asked her. Raquel nodded.

"Explain how you know that," I probed.

"Because the sides match," she said.

"That's right," I answered. "I don't think this one follows the rule," I said, pointing to her shape.

She looked at me wryly. "Nope," she pronounced, and returned to the triangles to search for a new shape.

Martha and Javier had completed *More Shapes on the Geoboard* and were discussing what to do next. I watched as they took out some green Pattern Block triangles.

"How many do we need?" Martha asked Javier.

They looked at the instructions and read them together. I remembered that both children had been absent when we did the whole group activity *Shapes with Pattern Block Triangles.* I was amazed at the independence they were demonstrating. These were not the same two children who had walked into the room last fall.

"What paper do we use?" Javier asked Martha.

"I don't know what we're doing anyway," Martha said, shaking her head. "What's the glue for?" Together, they figured out what to do. I watched how Martha organized the materials on the table in front of them. "Keep everything in order," she instructed Javier.

I returned to Antonio and Josie. They had cut several shapes out of the triangle paper and were ready to glue them down. I noticed that they had elected to add them to the same paper they had used for shapes made from four and five triangles. Josie carefully drew a line to delineate a new section, and labeled it *6's.*

I wanted to reinforce the decisions they had made. I said, "You put your shapes into clear categories and labeled them. That really helps me understand what you found out." Rather than saying "I like how you . . . ," I spoke specifically about how their decisions communicated clearly.

As I walked past Martha and Javier, I heard them talking about how to divide up the work. Martha said, "I'll make the shapes, and I want to glue them on. You cut them out." This seemed fine with Javier, and they began.

I checked up on Raul and Steve. They seemed to be working together well. They had found, cut out, and glued five different shapes and were searching for another. I didn't interrupt them.

I watched Raquel work. She had built three different shapes with the Pattern Blocks and was trying to cut them out of triangle paper. Raquel selected a shape and moved it next to the triangle paper. She seemed to be trying to visualize how the shape would look on the triangle paper. Raquel drew the shape onto the paper and began to cut, not following the lines.

NOTE Deciding whether to intervene and show students what to do or let them figure it out for themselves requires professional judgment. Giving help as a regular course of action risks disabling instead of enabling children. The more children learn to handle their own problems and answer their own questions, the more capable and confident problem solvers they can become.

Raquel really needed a partner for this activity, I reflected. I probably should have encouraged her to join another group. I worried that making the change now would give her the message that she wasn't capable. So I gave her a suggestion.

"Raquel," I said, "when you use triangle paper, you need to cut on the lines. Would it help if you actually put the shape on top of the triangle paper? Then you can trace it and it will follow the lines." I showed her what I meant.

Raquel nodded and did one herself. "Is this right?" she asked.

"It looks to me as if your shape does follow the lines," I answered. "What do you think?" Raquel agreed.

As I again walked past Martha and Javier, I saw that they had made shapes with three, four, five, and six triangles. This was fine with me, since they had missed the whole class lesson when the class explored shapes with three, four, and five triangles.

I saw Martha point to a hexagon and tell Javier, "This is like a hexagon." Martha had begun using the terminology I had been modeling.

Raul looked enthusiastic. I wondered what was going on, and walked over. Steve looked at me, "We're gonna get *another* one!" The boys had found six shapes, and Steve was cutting out a seventh. Steve examined the shape and snipped a triangle off.

Raul looked at the shape. "Hey, that's a different one you made. You messed up."

I made a mental note to have a class discussion about what makes a good partner. Raul needed to learn how to be supportive. But Steve seemed unaffected by Raul's criticism. He picked up the paper triangle he'd snipped off, went to get tape, and reattached it in a different place.

Raul and Steve proudly strutted across the room to announce to some friends, "We already have seven!"

After Paul and Steve figured out how to work together, they found nine shapes, two of which were congruent.

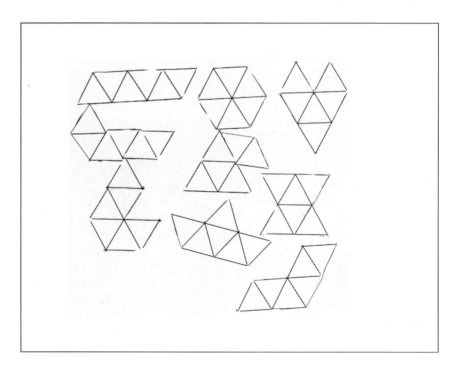

A Class Discussion

The previous day I had told the children that we would begin today's lesson by discussing *Shapes with Six Triangles.* Those who had not yet done the activity were to work on that first, and during the period all the children posted their work.

The children gathered on the rug, looking at the board where their work was posted. I began a class discussion with a general question, not one related specifically to this activity. "What makes someone a good partner?" I asked.

"They help you," Danny told us.

"And they're not mean," Linda added.

"What kinds of things do they do to help you?" I continued. I wanted the children to share specific examples of a positive nature.

"Well, like, they get the materials," said Adrian.

"What else?" I asked.

Martha had an idea. "They help cut things out and glue them," she said.

Martha pointed out that one person might do all the work and that wouldn't be fair. I asked her to explain how she and Javier had divided up the work. "We each had jobs," she said. Javier nodded.

Other groups also talked about how they had shared responsibilities. Because of this discussion, today we would have less time to talk about the mathematics in the activity, but that was fine with me. I find these discussions extremely valuable.

To move the discussion to the mathematical investigation, I asked, "What did you find out about six triangles?"

"There are eight shapes," Francisca said. She got up and pointed to her paper. She looked her partner, Adrian. "Right?" she asked. Adrian nodded.

"What shapes did you find?" I asked.

NOTE It's important to take time to discuss how children should work together. Learning to work collaboratively takes time and doesn't happen without guidance from the teacher. Class discussions about cooperating help focus students on options for working with one another.

Francisca and Adrian found eight different shapes by combining six triangles.

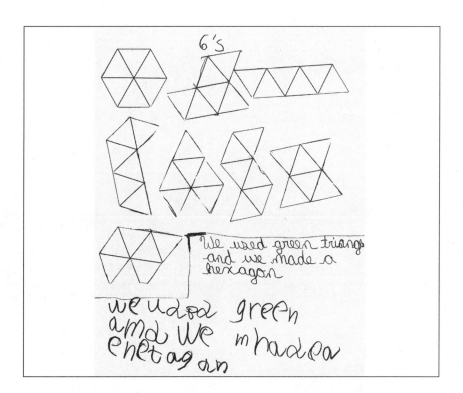

Francisca read what she had written: *"We used green triangles and we made a hexagon."*

"Are they all hexagons?" I asked, noticing Danny and Alejandra's paper, which had every shape labeled *hexa-6.* Francisca nodded as Steve said, "The straight one isn't."

"How do you know that?" I probed.

"It doesn't have six points," Steve explained. We counted the four corners and sides.

"It's a quadrilateral," I commented.

Danny and Alejandra arranged six triangles into six different shapes.

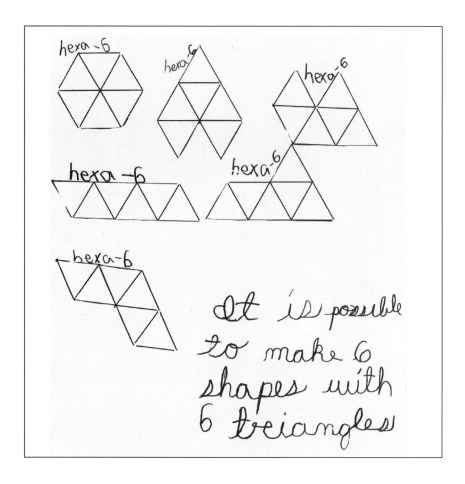

I moved on to ask another question, "How do you know that you found all the possible shapes?"

Danny said matter-of-factly, "That's all there is."

"Convince me," I said.

Alejandra said, "We tried and tried and tried and that's all there is."

Francisca pointed out that her paper had eight. "You forgot the candy cane," she said to Alejandra, getting up to point to a shape on her paper. Alejandra shrugged, seemingly not interested in Francisca's observation.

"How do you know that you and Adrian found all the shapes?" I asked Francisca.

Adrian explained, "I made a line of five and then I moved the other around it."

Francisca agreed. "That's all, because then we made a line of four and did the same thing." These children had found a system that worked for them.

It was lunchtime, and I asked the children to put their folders away.

"But we want to share," protested Josie. "We've been waiting and waiting."

I told her that she and her partner could share after lunch, and I made a note to myself so I'd remember.

Antonio and Josie made five different shapes with six triangles.

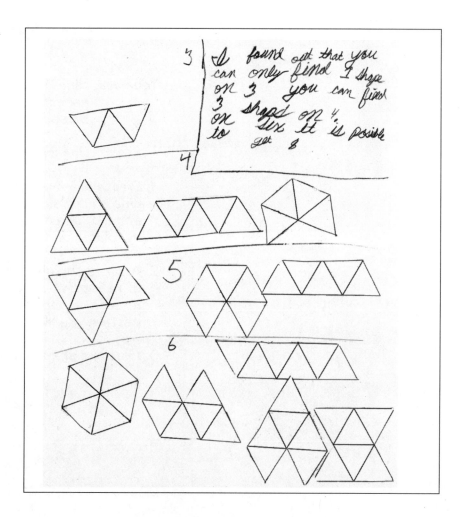

I wasn't concerned that the children hadn't found the 12 shapes. Children at this age are typically not able to find all shapes in a systematic way. However, by presenting their solutions and methods, even though they didn't exhaust all the possibilities, the children gained experience explaining their reasoning. This is a beginning stage in developing the ability to justify or prove solutions.

MENU ACTIVITY

Nine-Patch Patterns

Overview

In this activity the children use squares, cutting some of them in half to make triangles, to create nine-patch quilt patterns. As they examine the different shapes that appear in their patterns, children deepen their understanding of the properties of shapes and how they interrelate.

178

Nine-Patch Patterns   I

You need: Nine 3-inch squares of construction
        paper in two different colors
        Scissors
        Glue
        One 9-by-9-inch sheet of newsprint

1. Create a 3-by-3 square patchwork pattern using nine squares of construction paper. You can cut some or all of the squares in half into triangles by folding on the diagonal.

2. Arrange the shapes on the 9-by-9-inch sheet of newsprint, so the pieces do not overlap or go off the paper. Experiment until you find a pattern you like.

3. Glue the shapes down.

From *Math By All Means: Geometry, Grade 2* ©1994 Math Solutions Publications

Before the lesson

Gather these materials:

■ 3-inch squares of construction paper in a variety of colors (Each student will select nine squares in two colors, and additional squares will be needed for the homework assignment.)

■ One 9-by-9-inch newsprint square for each child*

■ Scissors

■ Glue

■ Blackline master of menu activity, page 178

*Note: It will help the children if the 9-inch newsprint squares are pre-folded into nine squares as shown.

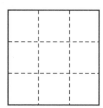

Do this by folding squares into thirds, opening then, and folding them into thirds the other way. It's quick and easy if you fold stacks of about eight squares each at one time.

Getting started

■ Tell the students that they will work individually to create quilt patterns. The patterns will be made up of nine squares, so they are called nine-patch patterns.

■ Explain that they will need nine squares in two different colors. Show them the supply of squares you cut. Discuss the possible numerical combinations of colored squares.

■ Tell the children that, if they'd like, they may cut squares in half into triangles, cutting only on the diagonal. Demonstrate for the children how to cut the squares by folding a square on the diagonal and cutting it along the fold. Add the word "diagonal" to the Geometry Words chart. Tell the children that they need to decide if they are going to cut some, all, or none of the squares into triangles.

■ Explain that they should place their squares and triangles on the newsprint square, making sure that the shapes neither overlap nor extend beyond the paper. The children should experiment until they find a pattern they like and then glue it in place.

■ For a class discussion, have the children post their patterns on the chalkboard. Begin by commenting on the variety and beauty of the patterns. Ask students what pictures and shapes they see in the patterns. Compare the patches: How are they the same? How are they different? Talk about the names of the shapes in the patches, using the Geometry Words chart for reference as needed. Choose a few designs and ask the children to figure out the number of squares of each color that was used in the designs. This question will challenge them to visualize how halves may be pieced together into wholes for some patterns.

■ Save the nine-patch patterns for the assessment *Shapes Inside Shapes* on page 131.

FROM THE CLASSROOM

"You're each going to design a quilt pattern using squares of colored paper." I showed the class the assortment of 3-inch squares of construction paper.

"You'll need a total of nine squares," I continued. "You can choose two different colors. What if you picked pink and purple? How many pink and how many purple squares could you use?"

Several hands shot confidently up. "18!" "17!" Apparently the children didn't understand my question.

I tried again. "You're telling me how many I'd have if there were nine pink and nine more purple. I'm asking a different question. I need nine squares altogether. I need a *total* of nine. How many could be pink and how many could be purple?"

The children began counting on their fingers. I waited until most hands were up. "18!" "18!" "19!"

Clearly, I had to use more than just words. I drew nine chalk squares on the board. "This is how many squares I need." We counted them. "Some can be pink and some can be purple. How many pink squares and how many purple squares could I use?" I had intended to tape the actual paper squares on top of the chalk squares, but the combinations were already being called out: "two pink and seven purple," "five purple and four pink," "eight purple and one pink," "eight pink and one purple," and so on.

I reminded myself of the importance of being concrete and breathed a sigh of relief at having finally communicated my meaning. But now I continued with this task. "Let's say I want five purple squares and four pink squares." The children helped me count them out. "For each square, I have to decide if I should leave the square whole or cut it. And the only way I can cut it is on the diagonal." I cut one square to demonstrate and wrote "diagonal" on the Geometry Words chart.

I picked up another square. "Should I cut it or leave it whole?" I did as the children suggested for three squares.

Then I held up a 9-by-9-inch newsprint square and explained that students would glue the squares onto that size paper. "The colored paper should not overlap or hang over the sides," I explained. I illustrated by holding the squares in those positions.

I gave one last direction: "Experiment with the colored shapes until you find a design you particularly like. Then glue the shapes in place."

Observing the Children

When the children began menu work, many chose to do this activity. I was interested in how they would approach selecting their nine squares. Alma chose two orange squares. She counted, "1, 2," and then counted on to 9 as she picked out seven red squares.

Jonathan announced, "I need three pink and six purple," quickly got his materials, and away he went. Stacy took more time. She selected a number of green and purple squares, then counted, removed, and recounted the squares until she was sure she had nine.

"What do we do?" Martha asked me.

I suggested that she either read the menu task or check with the other children at her table. "They can probably help you," I said.

I watched the children work. Raul used a ruler and a pencil to draw a diagonal line on a square to guide his cutting. He looked at the line, then shook his head and decided not to cut. He proceeded to lay all of his green and black squares on the newsprint. He arranged them and rearranged them. Finally satisfied with a checkerboard arrangement, Raul went to search for some glue.

Adrian picked up an orange square and cut it on the diagonal, by sight. He cut all of his orange and blue squares into triangles. Then he laid them out on his newsprint paper. He struggled to keep the triangles from extending beyond the edge of the paper. Turning and rotating the triangles, Adrian finally discovered that he had to put sides of the same length together.

I noticed that some of Danny's pieces overlapped. I reminded him that he needed to cover all the newsprint with his shapes and none of them could overlap. He seemed to understand.

Javier and Steve were sharing a bottle of glue. "Please hurry up," Javier said. I complimented Javier on his nice way of asking.

I saw that Adrian had put his triangles into a pattern. I asked him about it. Adrian explained to me, "It goes like this: blue-orange, blue-orange, blue-orange. Orange-blue, orange-blue, orange-blue."

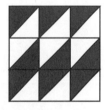

"You made orange and blue parallelograms," I told Adrian. I pointed them out on his patch.

Marcos had decided not to cut any of his blue and black squares. He tried a checkerboard pattern, then several others. He finally placed two blues on each side and formed a "T" with the black squares.

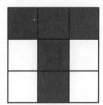

There was a quiet conversational hum in the room as children worked. Several proudly came to me to show me what they had made.

I looked at Martha's design. It seemed especially intricate, forming a diagonal X in the middle. I watched her struggle to fit the final triangle in the remaining space. The triangle kept extending beyond the newsprint. "It has to fit somehow," I encouraged her. Martha finally flipped her triangle over. It fit perfectly.

Later that afternoon I examined Martha's paper more closely. I realized that she had used only eight triangles, and thin lines of newsprint showed between them. No wonder her pattern looked very different from those the other children had made! I decided not to have Martha redo her design. Although Martha had not followed the directions completely, she'd had a rich geometry experience, creating smaller shapes from larger ones, and we worked hard to fit them back together in a design.

A Class Discussion

We displayed the quilt patterns on the board. "I think these are very interesting designs," I said. "Are any of them the same?" The children carefully examined the designs and decided that they were all different.

"What do the shapes in the designs remind you of?" I inquired.

"That one looks like a leaf falling down," observed Javier.

"And that one is half a house," said Amanda.

Alma commented, "That one looks like a face."

"Yeah!" added Jonathan. "I see the eyes!"

Alejandra had an idea. "Downtown they put a sign on the sidewalk for an advertisement, like 'Free Pizza.' It looks like that."

"This one looks like waves on the ocean," said Raquel. We all looked closely.

"No, it looks like a lady doing the splits," said Jonathan, and we all laughed.

One design reminded Martha of an activity we had done previously in the year. "The last one over here looks like an animal in the tangrams. It's like a duck to me, or a mosquito!"

"It reminds me of a strike of lightning," contributed Steve.

"What makes it look like lightning?" I probed.

"It points different ways," he answered, "like a zig-zag."

I chose one pattern to hold up. "What math shapes do you see in this design?" I asked.

"I see a pentagon," said Steve.

"How many sides and corners does it have?" I asked.

Steve counted the shape's four sides. "Oh!" he exclaimed, and went over to look at the *Hold and Fold* chart. "It's really a trapezoid," he decided, and I agreed with him.

I chose another pattern. "What shapes do you see here?" I asked. Voices chorused together, "A trapezoid! A trapezoid!"

Children came up one by one to show the group the different trapezoids that they found. "Lookit! There's a pink trapezoid! There's five now!" exclaimed Raquel.

"But look at this one," interjected Raul. "Here's a trapezoid made of two colors." Now with Raul's idea in mind, the children intently found more and more trapezoids.

I held up a different pattern. "What shapes do you see here?"

The children quickly found three more trapezoids. "Are there any other shapes?" I asked. Some of the children were so intent on finding shapes

NOTE Class discussions are extremely important for children's mathematical learning. Hearing other ideas and approaches helps children expand their own thinking. Also, when children articulate their ideas they are able to explore, clarify, and cement their understanding.

that they stood up and gathered around. I was pleased with their enthusiasm, but I asked them to sit down so all the children could see.

"It looks like teeth are shutting!" said Raul. "But what is that shape called?" He pointed to a parallelogram.

"It looks like a crystal," contributed Amanda.

We counted the four sides together. "It's a special kind of quadrilateral," I said. "The opposite sides are in the same direction, like railroad tracks, which makes them parallel. So the shape is called a 'parallelogram.'" I pointed to the word "parallelogram" on the Geometry Words chart.

I opened up a zip-top bag of Pattern Blocks. "Which of these do you think are parallelograms?" The children quickly discovered the two kinds of parallelograms, the blue and tan blocks.

I tried to get the children to verbalize their understanding of this shape. "How would you describe a parallelogram? What's it like?"

Raul said, "It has a square in the middle and two triangles on the end."

"It's like a diamond," said Martha.

"Here's another parallelogram!" cried Raul, and he leaped to his feet to point to another design. "And another! And here's another parallelogram!"

I went on to ask the children a new question, even though out of the corner of my eye I could see Raul whispering, "Parallelogram, parallelogram," as he continued to find them in the children's designs.

"When you made these patterns, you chose nine squares. You may have chosen three pink and six purple squares, or two red and seven orange squares. But they had to add up to nine." I held up Jonathan's design. "How many purple squares and how many pink squares did Jonathan use?" Jonathan had cut one of his pink squares on the diagonal and the two triangles were separated in his design.

"Three pink squares," Raquel said.

"How do you know?" I inquired.

"Two halves make one," she said, pointing to the two triangles, "then two, three," she said, pointing to the two pink squares.

"Do you agree?" I asked the rest of the children. It was interesting to watch the others mentally combine the triangles as they whispered numbers and pointed to Jonathan's design.

"If Jonathan used three pink squares, then how many purple squares did he use?" I asked.

The consensus was six. Some children came to that conclusion immediately. Some counted on their fingers. And others, like Elena, pointed to the shapes on the design, bringing their fingers together as they visualized two triangles coming together to make one square.

"How many orange squares did Elena use?" I asked.

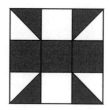

There was disagreement. Was it four or five?

Javier came up to share his thinking. "You have two big squares right there," he said, pointing. "And those triangles and those triangles make it four."

"What do you think?" I asked the group. "Are you convinced?"

They assured me they were, and I went on, "So if Elena used four orange squares, how many purple squares did she use?"

Again the children approached this problem in different ways, some figuring it out in their heads, others with fingers, and still others pointing to the design.

I was pleased at the way most of the children could visualize how to re-create the squares. But it was time for recess. I ended the lesson, gathering the quilt patterns to save for a later assessment activity.

ASSESSMENT Shapes Inside Shapes

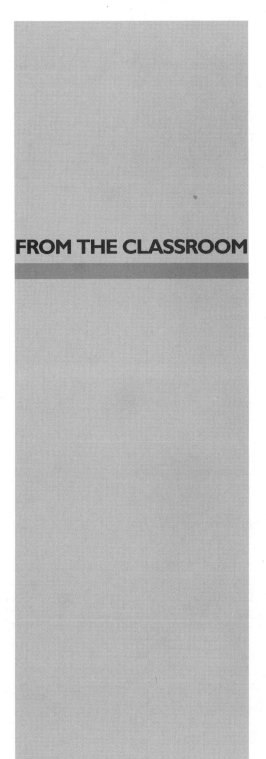

FROM THE CLASSROOM

This assessment is similar to the menu activity *More Shapes on the Geoboard* (see page 102), but instead of describing a single shape, the children describe shapes that they see within their nine-patch patterns. The assessment provides the opportunity to gain insights into how children perceive shapes within a design and the language they use to describe those shapes.

Review for the children that they have been exploring patchwork patterns for some time. They invented two patterns for cloaks and made a nine-patch quilt pattern. Explain that you would like them to write about the different shapes they see in their nine-patch patterns and about how they made those shapes. As with other written assessments, you might need to make adjustments for children's varied writing abilities; some children may need to use invented spelling, and others may need to dictate their thoughts.

The children's nine-patch patterns were posted on the board, and we had discussed them. (See the "From the Classroom" section of the menu activity *Nine-Patch Patterns,* page 126.)

"Now, I'd like to know what you can say about your own pattern," I told the children. "When you look at your design, you probably can see several shapes. I'd like you to work alone and write all you can about the different shapes that you notice."

I continued, "I'm especially interested in your explanations of how those shapes were made. For example, Javier made a trapezoid using four triangles. And Gabriel's hexagon is made from a square and two triangles."

Danny added to my explanation, "You can tell how the shapes connect."

"That would be fine," I said. "Write as much as you can, so I can get a good picture of what you think about when you look at your nine-patch pattern."

The children got down to work, some more quickly than others. Danny called me over to try to talk me out of having them work individually. He wanted us to make a group chart instead. "So we can gather more information," he assured me.

I smiled, but declined the suggestion. "This time I'm interested in finding out about each person's own ideas," I said.

Josie came to me. "I wasn't here that day," she said, explaining why she didn't have a pattern to write about. I suggested she share a pattern with someone else and write her thoughts on a separate sheet of paper.

"Will you help me write?" Antonio asked me. He looked frustrated, so I took dictation. Antonio talked about the pattern the squares made: blue, green, blue, green, blue, green.

"I'm done," Alejandra announced. She had written: *yo la hice con papelitos de cuadros despues la pege en un papel blanco luego le puse mi nombre.* (I made it with little paper squares then I glued it on a white paper then I put my name on it.)

"Alejandra," I said, "you've explained how you made your design. What I need now is to hear about the shapes you see in your design. What can you tell me about those shapes? How were they made?" Alejandra went back to work and added the following: *2 dos — la mia esta echa de puros cuadros bien suabe como los demas. 3 tres — yo veo en el papel*

Martha's paper shows how she has progressed in her use of geometric language and knowledge of the relationships between shapes.

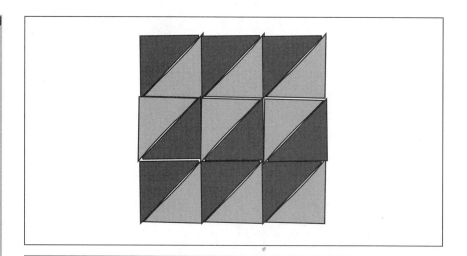

Nine Patch Patterns

I See a square and a triangle a dimohd
I uesd a squaresand a triangles and dimonds
triangles has for sides and a square has for sides to
I uesd 11 shapes to make a dosane. You could call the square and the triangle you cold call them quadrilaterials.
froma square to make a triangl you get a square and cut in the mitle and you have a triangle to make a dimond you trnea the square and you have a dimohd. to make a square you get a square.

una cruz una equis y una linia abajo. 4 cuatro — tambien veo que son como escaleritas de color anaranjado con verde. (2 two — mine is just made of squares it's really neat, just like the others. 3 three — on the paper I see a cross, an X and a line on the bottom. 4 four — I also see they're like little orange and green stairs.)

Javier had done more writing than usual, and was attempting cursive writing: *it looks lice a hexagon and a bol and a bowt made with 4 triyeangels.*

"I know more," he told me, so he dictated the rest: "I used nine squares of orange and blue. I got 19 triangles. And if you fold it you can make a Tuff-Shed." He showed me how he could fold his pattern so the orange trapezoids could touch and look like the storage sheds he had seen advertised.

Gabriel had an explanation for how he created his nine-patch design. Translation: *My shape has an octagon. Mine doesn't have a design. I put my family's initials on it and I only put the shapes any which way, then I glued them. My design is strange. Also I saw it was a rectangle. It's strange because it has hardly any shapes.*

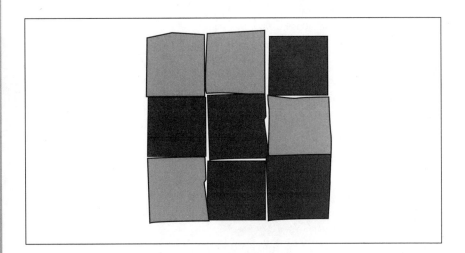

Mi forma tiene
un octugono
el mills ne tiene
un diseno yo le
puse las inisiales
de mi familia
yo nomas puse las
formas como sea.
y luego las page
mi diseno es extraño
tambien vi que eva un
rectangelo es exstraño porque
casi no tenia formas

nine patch
Patterns

Josie wrote: *The shapes are Triangles and Square. I nodice it made a hexagon. It was made with 2 Triangles and 1 square. I used Jonathan's pattern.*

Francisca explained how she had made her design: *I used nine squares to form my pattern that I chose to form. I notice that my color in my pattern that it is blue and blak and there is three blue and six blacks. Then the shapes were all squers not any other shape. I put black blue and I cept on*

Jonathan sketched his design, and found a twelve-sided shape in it.

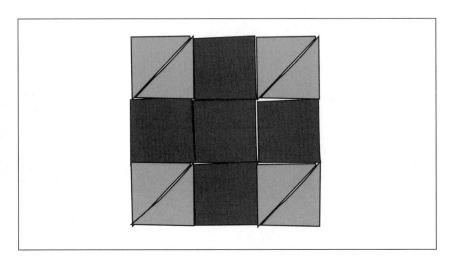

My Dezinc is a blue cros. The back round is yellow Triangles. My Dezinc has twelve sides. The cross has $ Five blue squars.

doing that until they were all used up and that is way there are three blue and six black. I put all the blacks in one row and blue in one row then black again. Then I put them together and found a rectangle with all of my shapes.

The children had seen a variety of things in their nine-patch designs. Several explained the repetitive patterns that they saw. Many children compared the shapes to things in the world around them. The class seemed to be using more of the standard shape names than before.

Steve found parallelograms and trapezoids in his design, and counted the yellow and blue triangles.

My disin has three parallelograms and six trapezoids and all together they make nine squares. There are six yollow traiangols and six blue taiangls and all together they are twelve. There are three hole squers.

MENU ACTIVITY

Overview

Shapes with Six Squares

This activity is an extension of the whole class lesson *Shapes with Pattern Block Triangles.* (See page 59.) The children create shapes by arranging six squares, following the rule that sides that touch must match completely. The children trace and cut out the shapes and tape them onto a class chart, checking to be sure that each shape they post is different from those already on the chart.

179

Shapes with Six Squares ⬚I

You need: 6 Color Tiles or orange Pattern Block
squares
1-inch squared paper
Scissors
Tape

1. Using the rule that sides that touch must match completely, arrange six squares into different shapes. Trace the shapes you make onto 1-inch squared paper. See how many shapes you can find.

2. Choose one of your shapes that is different from those already posted. Cut it out.

3. Test to make sure the shape has not been posted already. (Flip, rotate, and turn it to find out.) If it's different, tape it on the chart. If not, choose another shape, cut it out, and test it.

4. If you'd like, find other six-square shapes to post on the chart.

From *Math By All Means: Geometry, Grade 2* ©1994 Math Solutions Publications

Before the lesson

Gather these materials:
■ A minimum of six 1-inch squares (Color Tiles or Pattern Block orange squares) for each student (If possible, give each 12 squares. Then they can keep one shape built while experimenting with another.)
■ Blackline master, 1-inch squares, page 180
■ A large sheet of butcher paper or chart paper in a different color from the squared paper
■ Scissors
■ Tape
■ Blackline master of menu activity, page 179

Getting started

■ Explain to the children that they are going to make as many shapes as they can by putting together six squares, following the rule that sides that touch must match completely. (Demonstrate the rule if you feel it's necessary.) Tell students that they are to trace the shapes they make onto 1-inch squared paper.

■ Explain that students should choose one shape, cut it out, and tape it to the class chart. Before taping a shape on the chart, students should check to make sure the shape hasn't already been posted. Remind them that if a shape can match another by rotating or flipping, it's considered the same shape, or "congruent." If they'd like, they can post more than one shape, as long as each shape is different from those already on the chart.

■ Ask the children to predict how many different shapes are possible. (Note: Thirty-five shapes are possible, but do not reveal this to students. The goal of the activity isn't to have children find all the possible shapes but to encourage them to think about the variety of ways they can arrange six squares.)

■ In a class discussion, ask the students whether there are any duplicates on the chart. Remove duplicates and have the students count the number of different shapes on the chart. Ask them to name the shapes, referring to the Geometry Words chart as needed. Have them discuss whether they think all the possible shapes have been found. Compare the total number of shapes with six squares to the total number of shapes they found with six triangles. Ask them why they think these totals are different.

■ Leave the chart posted and encourage students to keep looking for shapes.

FROM THE CLASSROOM

"Remember how we put the green triangles together?" I asked the class. "There was a certain rule about how they could go together."

"I know," said Francisca. "The sides have to touch."

"They have to be even," added Stacy. She used some Pattern Block triangles to show how they had to match.

I told the students that in this activity they would make shapes with six squares, following the same rule. "How many shapes do you think are possible?" I asked. "Remember, shapes that match exactly when you turn or flip them are congruent and count as the same."

Javier raised his hand. "20 maybe. No, 16," he corrected himself.

"What made you change your mind?" I asked.

"20 just seems a lot," Javier said.

"Maybe 10," said Elena.

"Why do you think that?" I asked.

"Oh," she said, "we found eight for the triangles, and the square might have more." When I asked why she thought the square might have more, Elena shrugged her shoulders.

I continued with the directions. "You'll trace the shapes you make onto the paper with 1-inch squares," I said. The children nodded. The activity was just like the triangle problem they had already done.

I posted a chart on which the children were to tape their shapes. I used colored paper so that the shapes they cut from white paper would be easily visible.

"Choose a shape to post on the chart and cut it out. But only one of each possible shape should be posted," I explained. "So before you tape a shape on the chart, check to see that it's different from all the others already posted. If two shapes match, they're congruent, and only one should be posted. Compare your shape with the others to be sure it's different." Expecting each child to find a different shape is reasonable, because it's possible to make 35 non-congruent shapes using six squares. I didn't give the children this information but focused them on creating and comparing shapes.

I asked for a volunteer to label the chart "Shapes with Six Squares." Alma took the job. As much as possible, I have the children do chores like this. Many learning opportunities for children exist in the preparations that we teachers traditionally do in the classroom.

"If you choose this task," I explained, "you can use either Pattern Block squares or Color Tiles. It's an individual activity, which means you each have to post one shape, but you can post more than one shape if you'd like. Also, it's okay to work together." The children were aware of the option of working together, even on individual tasks, but I reinforced it just as a reminder.

Observing the Children

Francisca and Stacy sorted Pattern Blocks until they had a pile of orange squares, and then each began making different shapes with their squares. They worked separately, tracing and cutting out their shapes. They each posted two shapes on the chart and then returned to look for more.

A fairly constant stream of children walked to and from the chart, checking and posting shapes. Jonathan and Gabriel were at their seats working with Color Tiles. I watched Gabriel place his tiles on the paper, trace the shape, and cut it out. He went up to the chart. "Did anybody do the hammer?" he asked aloud.

Francisca was ready with a new shape and joined Gabriel at the chart. "It's already there," she said, showing him where the shape was on the chart. Gabriel returned to his seat to try again.

Francisca stayed at the chart to check her new shape. While she was looking over the other shapes, she found two shapes that were congruent and removed one of them. Martha joined her, a cut-out shape in her hand.

"Did someone already do this?" Martha asked.

Francisca peered at the shape. She wasn't sure. Martha counted the numbers of squares in each row of her shape, and began counting squares on the shapes posted to see if there was a match.

Amanda joined them at the chart, taped up her shape, and then counted the shapes that were posted. "13," she told me.

"How many do you think are possible?" I asked her.

"Maybe 17." Amanda's estimate was within the same range as Javier's. Having children find out the exact number of possible shapes wasn't a goal of this activity. I asked them to estimate only to see if they would have any idea about the number of possibilities after making shapes.

Meanwhile, Martha was satisfied that her shape was different and taped it to the chart.

I watched the children continue to search for new shapes. Steve was posting one with only four squares. "You need six," corrected Danny. I noticed another shape on the chart with only five squares and also one with seven. I asked Danny to check and remove shapes with other than six squares and post them next to the chart. I planned to call the children's attention to this when I talked to them at the end of the class so that I could remind them to be careful.

A Class Discussion

I called the class together a few days later for a class discussion. The children arranged themselves on the rug so that they all could see the chart. When I had their attention, I began. "Look at all the shapes you found!" I said. "What do you notice about them?" I asked.

"There's a bunch of letters," Martha said. "There's an L and an F and a T."

"*Two* Ts," corrected Gabriel, "an uppercase and a lowercase."

"And there are two Zs," Adrian said. "But they're not the same."

"There are two rectangles, exactly the same," Raquel noticed. "How'd that happen?" she wondered aloud as she came up to remove one.

"Any other duplicates?" I asked.

There was a silence as the children considered the shapes. Alejandra gazed, her head to the side, her fingers pointing at different shapes. "I think they're all different now," she said uncertainly.

"Do you agree?" I asked the class.

"They're all different," Danny said in his usual definite manner. The other children were nodding. I was about to have the class focus on two shapes that were congruent but positioned differently, one rotated and flipped.

Just then Elena spoke up. "The Zs are the same," she said softly.

"No, they're not," disagreed Danny.

"Yes, they are," Elena quietly insisted.

"Why do you think they're the same?" I asked Elena.

"It's got one square in the middle," she replied, "with a three and a two on the ends."

"But," countered Danny, "that one's got the three on the bottom and the other's got the three on the top."

"What could we do to find out if the shapes are congruent?" I asked the class.

NOTE It's important to maintain a safe environment in the classroom where children are free to take risks and try out ideas. Also, errors should be seen as opportunities for learning, not as unfortunate events.

"Take them off and put one on top of the other," Adrian told us. We followed his advice and found that, when one shape was flipped and rotated, it matched the other shape.

Neither the children nor I could find any other duplicate shapes. I continued the discussion. "I see a hexagon," I said. "Can anyone find it?"

A flurry of children counted sides and corners of different shapes. "I found it!" crowed Raul. He came up to show us, counting the L-shape's six sides as proof.

"How about an octagon? Can you find a shape with eight sides?" As the children searched and counted, I added "octagon" to our Geometry Words chart. The children found two different shapes with eight sides and eight corners.

I moved on. "Javier predicted we'd find 16 shapes and Elena thought maybe 10. Let's find out how many different shapes we really did find. How could we count them?"

The children have had many experiences counting sets of objects in different ways. "By 2s," suggested Steve.

Using a red marker, I circled the shapes in groups of two, ending up with 12 groups and one shape left over. "Turn to a friend," I instructed, "and together figure out how many shapes we have altogether." I wanted as many children as possible to be engaged in answering this question.

There was a murmur and the pointing of fingers as the children counted by 2s. "There are 25," said Alejandra, and the rest of the children agreed.

"How else could we count the shapes?" I asked.

"We could go 5, 10, 15, 20," Adrian said. So, with a different color marker, I circled the shapes in groups of five, ending with five groups of five. Together we counted by 5s, again arriving at 25. The children seemed convinced that there were 25 shapes on the chart.

I connected this experience to a similar activity, *Shapes with Six Green Triangles.* "When we used the green triangles, we found how many different shapes?" I asked. "Eight," said Francisca.

"I had six," Adrian told us.

"But when we used squares, we found 25," I continued. "Why do six squares make so many more shapes?"

Francisca looked at the chart thoughtfully. But it was Martha who said, "Squares have more sides so there are more ways to hook on." Several children looked at me blankly and some wiggled, ready to do something else.

It was time to stop. "I'm just not convinced that we found them all," I said. "Let's leave the chart up for a few days. When you have a chance, you might see if you can find any more shapes." I left this as an ongoing investigation that the children could engage in from time to time.

ASSESSMENT Shape Walk

Taking the class on a walk to identify shapes helps you assess children's awareness of shapes in the world around them, the characteristics they notice to identify shapes, and the language they feel comfortable using to name the shapes they find.

Read *Shapes, Shapes, Shapes*, by Tana Hoban, to the children. (See the Children's Books section, page 157.) Have students discuss the shapes they notice. Then take the class on a walk through the neighborhood or, if that is not possible, around the school. Prepare the children for the walk by telling them they are to identify the geometric shapes that they see and the objects in which they find them. Have the children keep notes—in the form of words, pictures, or sentences—for use during a class discussion about the shapes they find. As you walk with the children, note the knowledge that children demonstrate about different geometric concepts. For instance, you might make the following observations:

■ Do some children find shapes immediately? These children may be especially aware of geometry in their world.

■ Do any children have a flexible way to see shapes, noticing different shapes in the same object? These children may have particularly strong spatial abilities.

■ Do any children make connections between the shapes they see, comparing one shape to another or remembering a similar shape elsewhere?

■ What characteristics do children use to describe shapes (sides, corners, angles, lines, diagonals, and so on)?

■ Do children name a shape by comparing it to something else ("it's like a shoe"), or are they beginning to use standard geometric terminology (such as "hexagon")?

FROM THE CLASSROOM

I showed the children the book *Shapes, Shapes, Shapes* by Tana Hoben. We had looked at the book at the beginning of the unit, but the children were still curious and enthusiastic.

"Oh, cool!" "Shapes!" "Look at the triangles!" were some immediate responses. We read the book's title and the name of the author, and we looked at the pictures on the book's inside cover.

"There are a lot of circles," observed Stacy, and we counted the circles on the ring, bracelet, scissors, egg, buttons, and measuring cup.

"There's another circle," said Amanda, and she showed us the inside rim of the button.

We looked at different pictures in the book, spending more time on some pages and less time on others. The students smiled at the picture of the child sailing a toy boat. They wondered about the fruit on another page: Was it an apple? A kiwi fruit? They decided it must be an avocado.

The photo of a wall under construction inspired the most discussion. Danny pointed out the two triangles made by the spaces between the diagonal boards. Then Raquel said, "Look! Two little triangles!" and showed us where they were.

"If you look at the whole wall, there's a rectangle," Francisca told us. And I showed the children the pentagon that I saw. Before we were finished with that page, we had found a variety of pentagons, several kinds of trapezoids, and many different triangles.

"It all depends on how you look at it," observed Raquel.

I felt that it was time to start our walk, so I closed the book. "You noticed a lot of geometric shapes in this book," I said. "What geometric shapes do you think we can find in our neighborhood?"

"There must be rectangles," announced Javier.

"Why do you think so?" I asked.

"Because there were a lot in my house," he answered. Javier was remembering the homework assignment. (See page 161.)

Introducing the Assessment

I told the children that we would be going on a neighborhood walk to see what shapes we could find. "After our walk, we'll talk about what we saw," I explained, "so we need to record what we discover. You can use words, pictures, sentences, numbers—anything that will help you remember what you find."

Before class that day, I had made a booklet for each child by putting together two sheets of 8$\frac{1}{2}$-by-11-inch paper, folding them in half to 5$\frac{1}{2}$-by-8$\frac{1}{2}$ inches, and stapling them on the folded side. I gave the children sheets of paper for recording. We didn't have enough clipboards for everyone, so I improvised. Several children used pieces of cardboard, with a rubber band around the top to hold the paper.

As we walked out of the room, the children were already finding shapes. "Look!" said Steve, "the sink has a circle!" He pointed to the drain.

Martha found rectangles in the floor tiles.

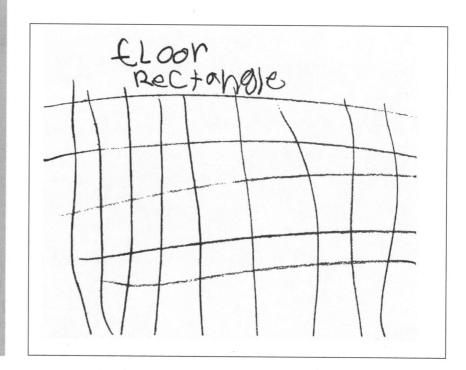

As we emerged from the building, the children immediately began to chatter. "Hey! I see triangles!" cried Martha, and she sat down to record the shapes on the banisters. Alma joined Martha to count them. "There are 13," Alma announced proudly.

"There's one right up there!" said Adrian, pointing to the triangle inside the large white letter "A" that graces a nearby hill.

Linda looked where Adrian was pointing and then carefully drew a triangle on her paper. "You might want to write something next to your triangle, so you remember what you saw," I suggested. Linda slowly wrote *mountin* next to her triangle.

The group slowly made its way down the street, pausing as children needed to record. Danny came over to me. "What's something with 10 sides?" he asked.

"It's a decagon," I answered, and spelled it for him.

Gabriel had decided that he wanted to find at least one of each geometric shape we had talked about in class. "I found another, so that's four," he announced. Gabriel's record sheet interested me. Below his original triangle, he had drawn a horizontal rectangle, a vertical rectangle, and another horizontal, but longer, rectangle. I was surprised that he had not grouped all the rectangles together.

Danny again wanted my attention. "Ms. Confer, the 'A' on the mountain has all these things: three rectangles and a triangle . . . No," he interrupted himself, "there's another rectangle. There are four!" Danny showed me the sketch he had made of the "A."

Danny found four rectangles in the "A" on "A Mountain."

In contrast to Danny's desire to talk and share, Raquel, Raul, and Linda were quietly recording what they noticed. I moved to where I could watch Raul. He had organized his paper in sections, labeling them *rectangle, triangle, five sides, square, seven sides,* and *circle.* Below each label Raul wrote the name of the object with that shape.

Gabriel said to me, "There's another shape," and he showed me the square spaces in a chain-link fence. He added a square to his list.

I heard Javier say to Martha, "Let me use your back for a second." Martha obliged as Javier drew a shape, finding it easier to draw from a higher stance.

I watched a group of children discuss what to call the back window of a Volkswagen van. "It's a rectangle, but its sides are like a circle," Danny explained.

"Then it's an oval," said Raquel.

"But it's too straight," countered Danny.

The flag on a mailbox also was the focus of a discussion. Javier counted its sides. "There are six," he announced. "What do you call that?" he asked Francisca.

"A hexagon," she supplied.

The children and I walked, talked, and wrote. I think it's valuable for me to be involved in the activities that the children do, to model and participate alongside them. My notes, however, also included my observations of things the children said and did, so I could later consider their geometry understanding.

All the children recognized and were interested in the geometric shapes in their world. They used their knowledge of geometry to represent and describe the neighborhood, each doing so in different ways.

At one point, I noticed more than half the class leaning against a wall, writing furiously. I had rarely seen them so anxious to write. They had clearly connected with this activity in an important way.

Linda and Raquel walked over to a shiny black truck to examine its window. As I approached the two, I heard them discussing what to call the shape.

"It has four sides," Linda told Raquel.

"It's got a slanty side," added Linda. "It looks like a shoe."

"A mathematician calls it a 'trapezoid,'" I said. "Have you seen that shape in any of our activities?" They thought so, but weren't sure where.

I noticed a group of children congregated around a sign on a store window. A number 4 had captured their attention and they were trying to categorize it.

"It has nine sides," crowed Danny, with his usual enthusiasm.

Javier double-checked. "Nope," he countered. "Try 11." I watched as they decided that Javier was correct.

Gabriel tugged on my sleeve, "Come look!" he said. "There's the fence that we saw in the book!"

The children had discovered a gate made of wood. The boards looked a lot like the frame wall that had attracted their attention in the book.

Alma pointed out a triangle that the boards made. "But look," added Raquel, "if you put this piece there too, you get five sides." She counted to show us.

Javier looked up at me. "What's that five-sided thing called?"

"It's a pentagon," Francisca said, rolling her eyes.

The children stood, pointing at different shapes and talking about them. I listened to a heated discussion between Danny and Javier.

"It's a *triangle*," emphasized Javier.

"No, it's not a triangle," countered Danny. He counted the five sides that he saw.

Javier was getting frustrated. "No, Danny, lookit! One, two, three."

Danny finally saw the shape Javier was referring to. "Well, I'm counting the wood in there," he explained.

"Well, I'm not," said Javier, hands on his hips. And he walked away.

I decided that it was time to return to the school. As we walked we chatted about the things we saw: a tall sunflower stretching toward the sky, a lizard lying still on a rock. And Gabriel found a 500-peso coin on the ground.

The children encountered more geometric shapes as they walked—in car emblems, a fire hydrant, seed pods, and a piece of broken glass. As we walked up the steps of the school, Danny voiced what was clear to us all, "Shapes are everywhere!"

Alejandra made notes and sketches about the shapes she saw as she walked.

A Class Discussion

After lunch, the children sat in a circle, recording booklets in hand, to share what they had discovered during our walk.

Raquel told about the rectangular license plate she had seen and a window made of rectangles. Several other children nodded that they had seen those things too.

"How did you record your observations?" I asked Raquel. She showed us the words she had written alongside her sketches.

Gabriel pursued his own question and looked for "all the different shapes."

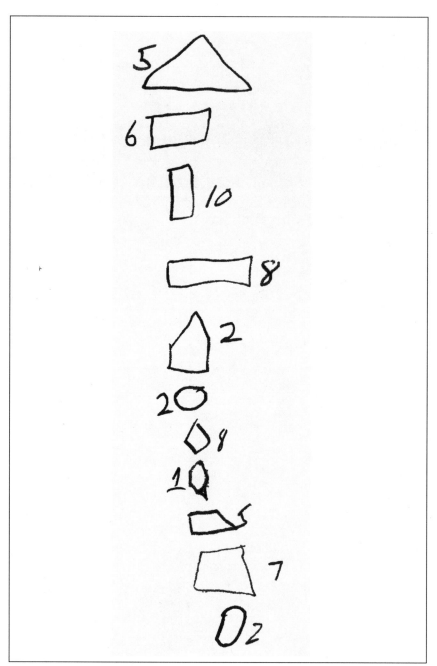

"I did the same thing," Linda told us. "Did you see the triangle fence?" she asked the group.

"It was made of wires," Elena contributed.

I asked Gabriel to share the results of his search for at least one of every geometric shape that we had talked about.

"I finished them," he said. Gabriel showed us his list of shapes and the number of each shape that he had found. I wondered what his method had been for keeping track of how many shapes he saw, as his paper only showed the totals. But the conversation had gone on without me. Gabriel was asking the others if they had also seen pentagons.

"I saw one on the stairs," offered Danny.

"That's a parallelogram," contradicted Javier in frustration. It seemed that their earlier disagreement was continuing.

"I can see how the two words are confusing. It can be hard to keep the names of the shapes straight," I said. "But what is most important to me is that Danny recognized the shape on our stairs. He remembered seeing the same shape, a parallelogram, on Raul's nine-patch pattern."

Observations

Later, I reflected on the experience. On our walk, I saw children demonstrate knowledge of different geometric concepts. I had been glad to hear quiet Raquel explain the different shapes she saw in the book's wall as well as her observation, "It all depends on how you look at it." Gabriel made an important connection when he found a similar fence in the neighborhood.

Danny had found a number of different shapes in the A on the mountain. He had a flexible way of noticing different shapes.

I had enjoyed watching the children deal with the atypical shapes they encountered, such as the rounded rectangular rear window of a Volkswagen van and the numeral 4 in a sign. The children knew that the shapes we'd been studying had straight sides and that they were named according to the number of sides.

I considered the geometric language I had heard. Francisca seemed to be proud of the mathematical terminology she could use (and not very patient with others who could not yet do so). Most children used shape names when they could and descriptive words ("five sides" or "like a shoe") when they couldn't.

I had wanted to set up a situation where I could watch children recognize and appreciate geometry in their world. Each child had done so. I was pleased by their enthusiasm as well as the variety of observations that they had made.

ASSESSMENT What Is a Triangle? (Revisited)

This assessment repeats an assignment that the students did at the beginning of the unit, thus giving an indication of how their ideas have changed. During the unit, the children have many experiences comparing shapes, manipulating shapes, constructing shapes, and taking shapes apart. They investigate shapes in the world around them. They also develop some knowledge of the language of geometry.

This assessment helps you look at several questions: What conceptions do the children have about triangles? Do they have any misconceptions? How have their perceptions changed over the course of the unit?

Ask the children once again to write a description of a triangle so that someone who has never seen one can picture it. They should include everything that they know about triangles: how they're made, what different kinds there are, how they relate to other shapes, and where triangles appear in our world.

FROM THE CLASSROOM

I explained to the children the purpose of this assignment. "We've been learning about geometry for almost six weeks now," I began. "We've done a lot of activities with shapes. We made triangles and other shapes on the geoboard, we put Pattern Block triangles together to make new shapes, and we cut a square apart and used the pieces like puzzle pieces. We've also used shapes to make different kinds of patchwork patterns." I pointed to the list of menu activities as I spoke.

"You all know what triangles are," I continued. Some students traced triangles in the air. "Do you remember when you wrote about triangles at the beginning of the unit? I'd like you to do the very same thing now. But since you've done so many new things with triangles, you'll probably have some new or different things to write."

I tried to emphasize the importance of the assignment. "I want you to write as much as you can about triangles. It will help me find out how the activities we did helped you learn about geometry."

I listed on the board some things for the students to think about as they wrote:

What does a triangle look like?
How are triangles different from one another?
How can you make a triangle from another shape?
Where in the world do you see triangles?

Martha asked, "Do we have to fill up the paper?"
"Everything that's in your head, you need to put on the paper," I answered. "When you've told me everything that you know about triangles, and you've thought about the questions on the board, then you're finished. You might fill up the paper, or you might not."

"Also," I added, "don't worry if you're not sure how to spell a word. Just do the best you can. And, you can use pictures if you want."

Carmen gave many examples of triangles in the world: A triangle has three sides and looks like a ring and also a window in a car and a piece of a pizza and a dog's ears and a cat's fingernails and also a letter and also little seeds.

Un triangulo es el que tiene tres lados y se parese a un anillo y tamen se parese a La vetana de un karo y a Los pedaso de una pisa pero a Las oregas de un pero y La uñas de Lo gatos y tamen un lera y tamen Las semillitas.

NOTE Partial understanding and confusion are part of the ongoing learning process. Children come to school with differing experiences, talents, interests, and rates of development. Assessments can identify differences and help teachers learn what children understand.

The children got their papers and sat down. Steve asked Raul, "What's a triangle? I forgot."

"You forgot what a triangle is?" asked Raul, aghast.

"It goes like this," said Jonathan matter-of-factly, and he used his finger to trace a triangle on the table.

"Oh, yeah," Steve said.

Some children got right down to work; others chatted a bit before starting. Alma looked confused. "Do you know what a triangle is?" I asked her. She answered yes and drew one in the air. I guessed she would sort it out for herself, so I moved on.

Adrian had written a sentence, but put down his pencil and sighed. I was sure he had more to say about triangles. "Would you like some help?" I asked him. Adrian sighed and nodded. He dictated what he wanted to say as I wrote his words.

As children finished and brought their papers to me, I asked them to read them aloud.

Amanda wrote about triangles in many ways: *A triangle is a shape that has three sides and three points. Its the shape of a pizza slice. You can make a triangle maney ways you can make it skinny or fat. You can make a big triangle with two small triangles a rectangle and one big triangle.*

Stacy began her paper with several examples of things in the world that have triangular shapes.

A triangle is a cut shape like the letter A and top of a house. The shape of the points of a star even the birds beack. It has 3 sides and 3 points, If you cat a square dieagualy it will turn out to be two triangles, It is the shape of a pencial led.

Francisca described several attributes of triangles. Then she noted that a triangle may be rotated and still be the same shape.

A triangle is a shape with three sides. It has one ponit on the top of the triangle then it has two ponits at the bottom of the triangle. But if you turn it around you can find that you have the same triangle but at different angles but it is still the same triangle shape to it. The color of the triangles can be any color you want them to be you can make them Orange or red or any color you want.

Alejandra wrote: *Un triangulo tiene 3 lados es como un pedaso de pizza porque tiene 3 lados tambien las orejas del gato tiene un triangulo. Los triangulos son grandes y chiquitos todos los triangulos son diferentes.* (A triangle has 3 sides. It's like a piece of pizza because it has 3 sides. A cat's ears also have a triangle. Triangles are big and small. All triangles are different.)

Linda had written laboriously: *a triangle has like a tip of a castle.*

Martha demonstrated her new understanding that a triangle can be positioned differently and still be a triangle. She wrote: *A triagle has 3 sides and 3 cornrs and it is little. It looks lik a yield sine. Evan you turnd a triagle around it will still be a triagle.*

Several children showed how a triangle can be cut from a larger shape. Danny wrote: *A triangle is a shape like the letter A and the top of a castle and a House. A beak of a bird is a triangle. A triangle has 3 sides. If you cut a square diagonaly it will make two triangles.*

Gabriel explained about triangles through a story: *Mi hermanita no save que es un triangulo. Cuando yo estoy asiendo las matematicas mi ermanita quiere aser dibujos y mi mama le dise dibuja un triangulo. Yo le digo un triangulo es como una esquina de una mesa. O una mitad de una cama cortada en diagonal. Le digo el triangulo tiene tres lados y le enseño a dibujar un triangulo.* (My sister doesn't know what a triangle is. When I'm doing math, my sister wants to make pictures and my mom tells her to draw a triangle. I tell her, "A triangle is like a corner of a table. Or a half of a bed, cut on the diagonal." I tell her that a triangle has three sides and I teach her to draw a triangle.)

CONTENTS

CHILDREN'S BOOKS

Children's picture books have long been one of teachers' favorite tools for nurturing students' imaginations and helping them develop an appreciation of language and art. In the same way, children's books that have a connection to mathematics can help students develop an appreciation for mathematical thinking. They can stimulate students to think and reason mathematically and help them experience the wonder possible in mathematical problem solving.

Each children's book described in this section can add a special element to one or more of the activities in the geometry unit.

Brian Wildsmith 1 2 3
by Brian Wildsmith
Oxford University Press, 1987

This simple counting book uses shapes to illustrate quantities. Many shapes are divided in intriguing ways. A good springboard to discussions about smaller shapes inside larger shapes.

A Cloak for the Dreamer
by Aileen Friedman
illustrated by Kim Howard
A Marilyn Burns Brainy Day Book, 1994
(Available from Cuisenaire Company of America)

Three sons work for their father, a tailor. Each son is asked to sew a colorful cloak for the Archduke. The first son sews together rectangles of fabric to make his cloak. The second son sews together squares and then makes a second cloak from triangles. But the third son, a dreamer, uses circles, making a cloak full of holes. The father finds a (geometric) way to repair the dreamer's cloak. This book provides the basis for the whole class lesson by the same name. (See page 42.)

Color Zoo
by Lois Ehlert
J.B. Lippincott, 1989

Color Farm
by Lois Ehlert
J. B. Lippincott, 1990

Each of these books has vivid, striking illustrations of animal faces formed by overlays showing different combinations of shapes. The books invite the children to combine shapes and invent new animal faces.

Ed Emberley's Picture Pie
by Ed Emberley
Little, Brown and Company, 1984

Emberley describes how a circle divided like a pie can be used to create myriad designs, pictures, and patterns.

Eight Hands Round: A Patchwork Alphabet
by Ann Whitford Paul
HarperCollins Publishers, 1991

This delightful book talks about the importance of patchwork quilts during the first 100 years after the signing of the Declaration of Independence. It shows 26 different patchwork patterns and how each pattern might look with pieces sewn together into a quilt. The book also describes aspects of colonial life. A good introduction to the culminating activity *Quilts from Nine-Patch Patterns.* (See page 69.)

Fishy Shape Story
by Joanne and David Wylie
Children's Press, 1984

Colorful illustrations introduce shapes by showing fanciful fish of different shapes. This amusing story ends with the child imagining a fish decorated with all of the shapes. (Available in Spanish: *Un Cuento de Peces y Sus Formas,* translated by Lada Josefa Kratky; Dr. Orlando Martinez-Miller, consultant; Children's Press, 1986.)

The Greedy Triangle
by Marilyn Burns
illustrated by Gordon Silveria
A Marilyn Burns Brainy Day Book, 1994
(Available from Cuisenaire Company of America)

A triangle, dissatisfied with only three sides and three angles, goes to a shapeshifter to be changed to a quadrilateral. Later, the shape changes to a pentagon, then a hexagon, a heptagon, and so on, finally learning that being a triangle is best after all.

The Josefina Story Quilt
by Eleanor Coerr
Harper and Row, 1986

This book describes the exciting adventures of Josefina as her family moves West in a covered wagon. Josefina makes a patch for each event during their journey. When the family reaches California, Josefina sews the patches together into a story quilt.

Jugando con la Geometría
by Margarita Robleda Moguel
Sistemas Técnicos de Edición, S. A. de C. V., 1992

A circle, triangle, and rectangle play together, creating a rocket, a pencil, an ice cream cone, and other items. The shapes begin to argue about who is the most important shape, but they learn finally that all three shapes are equally important and that together they can have the most fun of all.

The Keeping Quilt
by Patricia Polacco
Simon and Schuster, 1993

This book tells the powerful story of a quilt passed down through four generations of women. The quilt marks important family events—births, weddings, a death—and binds the women together through the years. The baby born at the end symbolizes the continuing connection to future generations.

The Patchwork Quilt
by Valerie Flournoy
Dial Books, 1985

Tanya's grandmother begins a quilt made from pieces of the family's old clothes, scraps from a Halloween costume, and a special dress. As Grandma stitches the quilt, Tanya and her mother learn the joys of quilting. Grandma becomes ill, and Tanya takes over work on the quilt. Finally, Grandma is well enough to finish the quilt, which the whole family treasures.

El Reino de la Geometría
by Alma Flor Ada
illustrated by José Ramón Sánchez
Laredo Publishing Company, 1993

This is a nice introduction to tangrams, written in Spanish. Peace reigns in the Kingdom of Geometry until King Square VII decides that the square is the perfect shape. The other shapes are discriminated against, until they learn that they can combine themselves to make squares and other designs. The shapes decide to move away; they don't need a king after all.

Sam Johnson and the Blue Ribbon Quilt
by Lisa Campbell Ernst
Lothrop, Lee, and Shepard Books, 1983

Sam discovers the pleasures of quilting but learns that he is not welcome in the women's quilting club. The local men begin their own club, and when disaster strikes, the two groups find a solution by making a quilt together.

The Secret Birthday Message
by Eric Carle
HarperCollins, 1986

Tim has a secret message that leads him to his birthday present by using shape clues. Then, at the end of the story, a map illustration retells the story using the clue words and the shape names.

The Shapes Game
pictures by Sian Tucker
verse by Paul Rogers
Henry Holt and Company, 1990

Bouncy, rhythmic riddles and lively illustrations celebrate the shapes in a child's world. The shapes include squares, circles, triangles, ovals, crescents, rectangles, diamonds, spirals, and stars.

Shapes, Shapes, Shapes
by Tana Hoban
Greenwillow Books, 1986

Colorful photographs of everyday objects show children the many different shapes in the world around them.

The Tangram Magician
by Lisa Campbell Ernst and Lee Ernst
Harry N. Abrams, Inc., 1990

A magician decides to change himself into different creatures. Bold tangram designs depict his transformations. The book invites readers to use the pressure-sensitive vinyl stickers found inside the book to re-create the illustrations and to make their own designs.

Texas Star
by Barbara Hancock Cole
Orchard Books, 1990

Winter is coming, and Mother has a quilting party, complete with piles of food. The quilters finish a Texas Star quilt, which keeps the family warm as the winds howl outside.

CONTENTS

HOMEWORK

Homework has two purposes: It allows children to revisit a topic or concept that they considered during the school hours, and it lets parents see what their children are learning at school.

Children disappear from their parents' sight in the morning and reappear in the afternoon. Parent inquiries such as "How was school today?" or "What did you do at school?" often get the responses "Fine" and "Nothing." Homework that relates to the children's school experiences provides an important connection between the school and home. Parents can see what their children have been doing and have opportunities to participate meaningfully in their children's education.

Most parents have not had the kind of mathematics instruction presented in this unit. Although parents truly want what is best for their children, they often do not know what this means in a world of increasing complexity and rapid technological advances. Relevant homework, with an accompanying explanation of the work's rationale, can help provide this information.

Six homework assignments are suggested. Each is presented in three parts:

Homework directions

This section explains the assignment and includes organizational suggestions when needed.

The next day

This section gives suggestions for using the assignment in the classroom. It's important that children know that work done at home contributes to their classroom learning.

To parents

A note to parents explains the purpose of the homework and the ways they can participate in their child's learning. These communications help parents understand more fully their children's math instruction.

HOMEWORK   Search for Squares

Homework directions

Give this assignment anytime during the unit. (Asterisks in the Daily Schedule on pages 10–13 suggest possible days for giving the assignment.) Tell the children that they are to look for things at home that have squares or are made of squares. Have them predict the number of squares they think they'll find. Tell them to record what they find by writing or drawing pictures. If possible, they can bring actual objects to class.

The next day

Have the children share their discoveries. Discuss how they knew objects were squares. Were they surprised by the number of squares they found? Write the names of the objects next to the word "Square" on the Geometry Words chart. If the children brought actual objects, begin a class display of geometric shapes. Label this section "Squares."

To parents

> Dear Parent,
> It's beneficial for children to see how geometry is a part of their own world. Tonight the children are to look for things at home that are squares or have squares in them. You may want to join your child in this investigation. Your child should keep a record by writing or drawing pictures. If possible, he or she can bring actual objects to school. We will make a class list of what the children found. Also, we'd like to add to our class display any objects that the children bring to class.

HOMEWORK   Hold and Fold

Homework directions

Give this assignment after the children have done the whole class lesson *Hold and Fold*. (See page 34.) Each child takes home his or her specially folded 4¼-inch square and newsprint record sheet. This sheet shows all the different shapes the child made by folding the square only along the fold lines. The children help their parents fold these same shapes and name them. Then they check to see if they can find any other shapes. You may want to have the parents sign the paper and write a comment about the experience.

The next day

Have the children talk about the experience. With whom did they work? Were any shapes easier to find than others? Did anyone find new shapes to add to the class chart?

To parents

Dear Parent,
The children have explored the different shapes they can make by folding a square along only certain fold lines. They traced and labeled all the shapes they found. This activity helps your child understand relationships between geometric shapes and the language used to describe those shapes.

Please ask your child to help you fold all the shapes the class found. Read together the geometric name for each shape. See if you think the class found all the possible shapes. (Remember to fold only on the fold lines.)

HOMEWORK

Search for Rectangles (that aren't squares)

Homework directions

The children continue in their search for shapes at home by looking for rectangles. Give this assignment anytime during the unit. (Asterisks in the Daily Schedule on pages 10–13 suggest possible days for giving the assignment.) Since squares are special kinds of rectangles (with sides of the same length), state that they'll be looking for rectangles that are not squares. Have the children predict how many rectangles they think they will find at home. Again, the children may write the names of the objects, draw pictures, or bring actual objects for the class display.

Gabriel drew and labeled the rectangles he found at home: in a refrigerator, a door, windows, a bedspread, a curtain, a bed, a bus, and a table.

The next day

Have the children share what they found and explain how they knew that the objects were rectangles. Write the names of the objects next to "Rectangle" on the Geometry Words chart. Label a section of the class display "Rectangle" and add the rectangular objects students brought in.

To parents

Dear Parent,
For this homework assignment, your child will continue exploring geometry at home. Please have your child look for rectangles that are not squares. (A square is actually a special kind of rectangle with all sides the same length.) Your child may choose to write the words, draw pictures, or bring actual objects to add to our class display.

HOMEWORK

Search for Triangles

Homework directions

The children look for triangles at home. Give this homework assignment after the first *What Is a Triangle?* assessment or after the whole class lesson *Triangles on the Geoboard.* (See page 49.) (Asterisks in the Daily Schedule on pages 10–13 suggest possible days for giving the assignment.) Ask students to look for things at home that are triangular in shape or have triangles within them. Discuss the following questions: Do the children think there are many triangles at home? Will they find many different kinds of triangles, as they found on the geoboard? The children may write the names of the objects, draw pictures, or bring actual objects to school for the class display.

The next day

In a class discussion, have the children share the objects they found and explain how they knew they were triangles. Were the children surprised by the number of triangles that they found? Add the children's discoveries to the Geometry Words chart and the class display.

To parents

Dear Parent,
Please continue helping your child look for shapes at home, this time by searching for triangles. Your child may choose to write the words, draw pictures, or bring in the actual object for our class display.

Steve found several rectangles at home but only two triangles.

```
bed |          ⬜
door |         ▯
drows |        ▭
Closet door |  ▯
Picture fram|  ▯  ▭
Refregerater |    ▭
Picture |      ▱

Pennet |       ◁
kite |  |      ◺
```

thats all I have thats triangle in my house.

HOMEWORK

Search for Hexagons

Homework directions

The children look for hexagons at home. Ask the students to predict how many hexagons they will find. They may write the names of the objects, draw pictures, or bring actual objects to display. Give this assignment after you read *A Cloak for the Dreamer*. (See page 42.)

The next day

The children share what they found, explaining how they knew the shapes were hexagons. Ask them to discuss whether they were surprised by the number of hexagons they found. List the objects next to "Hexagon" on the Geometry Words chart. Label a section of the class display "Hexagons" and add any objects the students brought in.

To parents

Dear Parent,
Your child will continue exploring geometry in the world by looking for hexagons at home. Please feel free to join your child in this search for six-sided shapes. Your child may choose to write the words, draw pictures, or bring actual objects for display in our classroom.

Francisca found hexagons at her house.

> ① A rock in my front yard is a hexagon.
> ② A little knobe on my moms front of her car is a hexagon that you can twised
> ③ The inside of the steriny weel is a hexagon because it is shaped different but it has six sides still.

HOMEWORK

Homework directions

A Class Quilt

Give this assignment after the children have worked on the menu activity *Nine-Patch Patterns*. (See page 124.) The children make a new quilt pattern by taking home a 9-inch square of newsprint and nine 3-inch squares of construction paper in two colors. They work with a parent to design a nine-patch pattern, either leaving the 3-inch squares whole or cutting them on the diagonal. They make nine square patterns and glue them onto the newsprint to create a quilt square for a larger class quilt. You may wish to have the children figure out how many squares the teacher needs to cut so that each child can take home nine squares.

The next day

Ask the children to post their squares and then have the class decide how to lay out the quilt. Discuss the following: Is there a way to use all the squares and have a rectangular quilt? How should each square be rotated?

Tape the squares together and enjoy the beauty of your class quilt! Ask the children: What do you especially like about it? What shapes do you see in it? Would you like to give it a name, as the quilts in *Eight Hands Round* were named?

To parents

> Dear Parent,
> The children have been making patchwork patterns to learn how shapes relate to one another. For homework, your child is to work with you to make a nine-patch pattern. You will use nine small squares, which you may cut in half into triangles by cutting on the diagonal. (You can cut some, all, or none of the squares.) Experiment until you find a 3-by-3 pattern you both like. Then glue it to the newsprint. We will combine these patterns to make a class quilt.

CONTENTS

BLACKLINE MASTERS

The blackline masters fall into several categories:

Geometry Menu

This blackline master lists the titles of all the menu activities suggested in the unit. You may choose to enlarge and post this list for a class reference . Some teachers fill in the boxes in front of each title once they have introduced the activity, then students choose activities to do during menu time. Also, some teachers have children copy the list and make check marks or tallies each day to indicate the tasks they worked on; other teachers duplicate the blackline master for each child or pair of students.

Menu Activities

Seven menu activities are included. (Directions for the activities also appear following the "Overview" section for each menu activity.) You may enlarge and post the menu tasks or make copies for children to use. (Note: A set of classroom posters of the menu activities is available from Cuisenaire Company of America.) Blackline masters for shapes and patterns needed for several activities are also included.

Recording Sheets

Three blackline masters provide recording sheets for activities. Duplicate an ample supply of each and make them available to students.

Geometry Menu

☐ Rocket Shapes

☐ Square Designs

☐ Cloak Patterns

☐ More Shapes on the Geoboard

☐ Shapes with Six Green Triangles

☐ Nine-Patch Patterns

☐ Shapes with Six Squares

Rocket Shapes

P

You need: Four paper pieces, the same as for the rocket lesson

1. Use all four pieces to make each of these shapes: square, triangle, rectangle, hexagon.

2. Trace around each piece to show how you put the pieces together to make each shape. Label the four shapes you make.

3. Create a shape of your own with all four pieces. On a separate sheet of paper, trace just its outline, not the outline of each piece. Put your name on your shape and post it. If you want, make other shapes.

4. Try to fit your four puzzle pieces into other students' shapes. When you do so, sign your name on the back of the paper that shows the shape.

From *Math By All Means: Geometry, Grades 1–2* ©1994 Math Solutions Publications

Square Designs

P

You need: 4 1/4-inch newsprint squares
           Scissors
           Glue
           White or colored paper

1. Choose design A, B, or C.

2. Cut your paper square into four pieces and put them together into the exact same size and shape as the design you picked. (You might need to try several times.)

3. Glue your design onto white paper.

4. Follow steps 1, 2, and 3 for the other two designs.

5. Choose one of your three designs. Write about how you cut your square to make that design.

From *Math By All Means: Geometry, Grades 1–2* ©1994 Math Solutions Publications

Square Designs Shape A

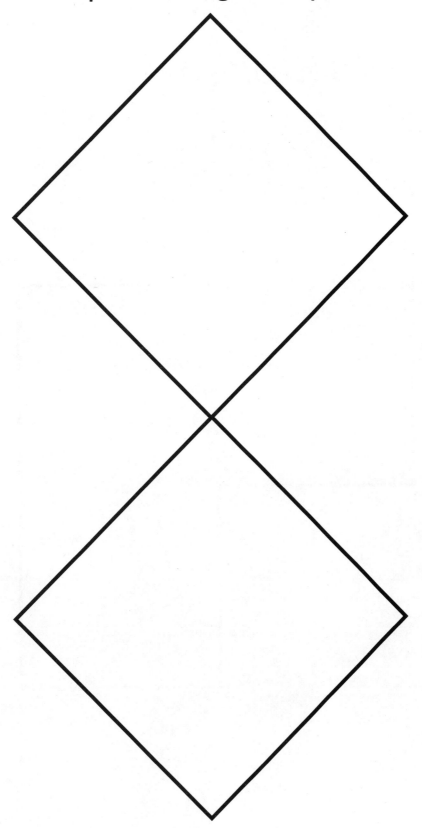

Square Designs Shape B

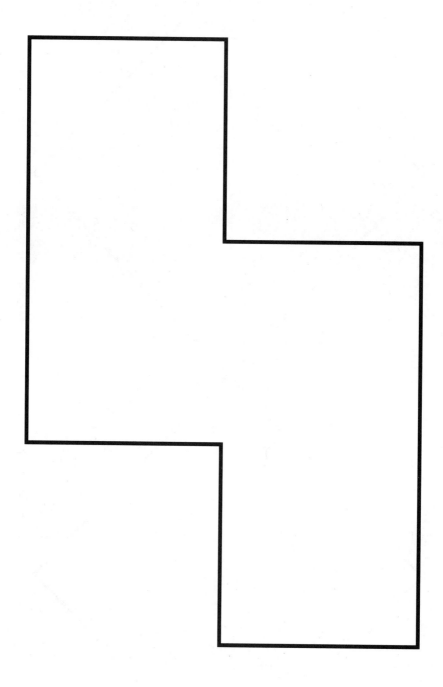

Square Designs Shape C

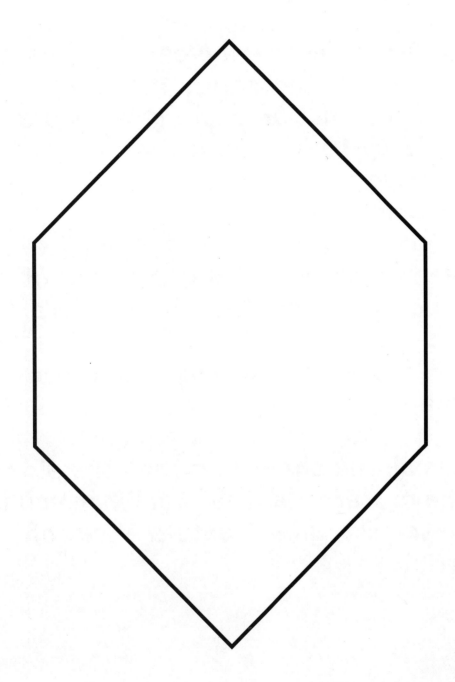

Cloak Patterns

You need: Two different tagboard shapes
           (square, rectangle, or triangle)
           Construction paper (two colors)
           12-by-18-inch newsprint
           Glue
           Scissors

1. Choose two shapes and two colors of construction paper. Using both colors, trace and cut out four to eight pieces of each shape. You can cut shapes in whatever color combinations you like.

2. Arrange all the shapes so that the sides match and the pattern pleases you. When you have a design you like, glue it onto a sheet of newsprint.

From *Math By All Means: Geometry, Grades 1–2* ©1994 Math Solutions Publications

A Cloak for the Dreamer Shapes

More Shapes on the Geoboard $\boxed{\text{I}}$

You need: One geoboard
One rubber band
Dot paper
Scissors
Tape or thumbtacks for posting

1. Make several different shapes on the geoboard. Each shape must follow these rules:

   - It must be made with one rubber band.

   - The rubber band must not cross over itself.

   - The shape must stay in one piece when you cut it out.

2. Choose one of your shapes. Make sure that it's different from those already posted.

3. Copy the shape onto dot paper and cut it out. Write your name on the back and post it.

Geoboard Dot Paper

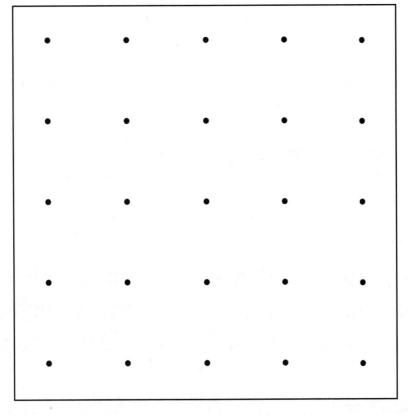

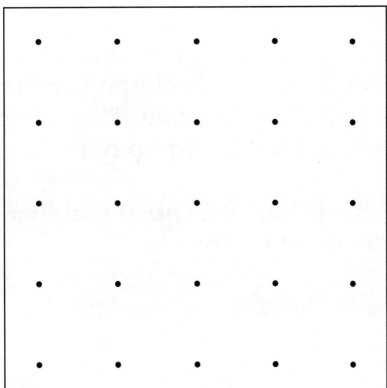

Shapes with Six Green Triangles P

You need: 12 green Pattern Block triangles
Triangle paper
Scissors
Glue
One sheet of colored paper

1. Using the rule that sides that touch must match completely, make as many different shapes as you can with six triangles.

2. Draw each shape you find on triangle paper and cut it out.

3. Test to make sure each shape is different by trying to match it to each other shape. (Flip, rotate, and turn it to find out.)

4. Glue all the different shapes you find onto a sheet of colored paper.

5. Write about the shapes you found.

Triangle Paper

From *Math By All Means: Geometry, Grades 1–2* ©1994 Math Solutions Publications

Nine-Patch Patterns $\boxed{\text{I}}$

You need: Nine 3-inch squares of construction
paper in two different colors
Scissors
Glue
One 9-by-9-inch sheet of newsprint

1. Create a 3-by-3 square patchwork pattern using nine squares of construction paper. You can cut some or all of the squares in half into triangles by folding on the diagonal.

2. Arrange the shapes on the 9-by-9-inch sheet of newsprint, so the pieces do not overlap or go off the paper. Experiment until you find a pattern you like.

3. Glue the shapes down.

From *Math By All Means: Geometry, Grades 1–2*   ©1994 Math Solutions Publications

Shapes with Six Squares   I

You need: 6 Color Tiles or orange Pattern Block
 squares
 1-inch squared paper
 Scissors
 Tape

1. Using the rule that sides that touch must match completely, arrange six squares into different shapes. Trace the shapes you make onto 1-inch squared paper. See how many shapes you can find.

2. Choose one of your shapes that is different from those already posted. Cut it out.

3. Test to make sure the shape has not been posted already. (Flip, rotate, and turn it to find out.) If it's different, tape it on the chart. If not, choose another shape, cut it out, and test it.

4. If you'd like, find other six-square shapes to post on the chart.

From *Math By All Means: Geometry, Grades 1–2*   ©1994 Math Solutions Publications

1-inch Squares

From *Math By All Means: Geometry, Grades 1–2* ©1994 Math Solutions Publications

Nine-Patch Pattern Samples

Ohio Star or Variable Star

Maple Leaf

Nine-Patch Pattern Samples

Churn Dash

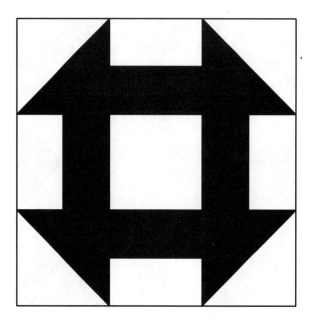

Letter X

BIBLIOGRAPHY

*Burns, Marilyn. *About Teaching Mathematics.* Math Solutions Publications, 1992.

*Burns, Marilyn. *The Greedy Triangle.* Illustrated by Gordon Silveria. A Marilyn Burns Brainy Day Book. Scholastic, 1994.

Carle, Eric. *The Secret Birthday Message.* HarperCollins Publishers, 1986.

Coerr, Eleanor. *The Josefina Story Quilt.* Harper and Row, 1986.

Cole, Barbara H. *Texas Star.* Orchard Books, 1990.

Ehlert, Lois. *Color Farm.* J. B. Lippincott, 1990.

Ehlert, Lois. *Color Zoo.* J. B. Lippincott, 1989.

Emberley, Ed. *Ed Emberley's Picture Pie.* Little, Brown and Company, 1984.

Ernst, Lisa Campbell. *Sam Johnson and the Blue Ribbon Quilt.* Lothrop, Lee, and Shepard Books, 1983.

— and Lee Ernst. *The Tangram Magician.* Harry N. Abrams, Inc., 1990.

Flournoy, Valerie. *The Patchwork Quilt.* Dial Books 1985.

*Friedman, Aileen. *A Cloak for the Dreamer.* Illustrated by Kim Howard. A Marilyn Burns Brainy Day Book. Scholastic, 1994.

Hoban, Tana. *Shapes, Shapes, Shapes.* Greenwillow Books, 1986.

Moguel, Margarita Robleda. *Jugando con la Geometría.* Sistemas Técnicos de Edición, S. A. de C. V., 1992.

National Council of Teachers of Mathematics. *Curriculum and Evaluation Standards for School Mathematics.* National Council of Teachers of Mathematics, 1989.

*Paul, Ann Whitford. *Eight Hands Round: A Patchwork Alphabet.* HarperCollins Publishers, 1991.

Polacco, Patricia. *The Keeping Quilt.* Simon & Schuster, 1993.

*Rogers, Paul. *The Shapes Game.* Illustrated by Sian Tucker. Henry Holt and Company, 1990.

Wildsmith, Brian. *Brian Wildsmith 1 2 3.* Oxford University Press, 1987.

Wylie, Joanne and David. *Fishy Shape Story.* Children's Press, 1984.

Wylie, Joanne and David. *Un Cuento de Peces y Sus Formas.* Translated by Lada Josefa Kratky; consultant Dr. Orlando Martinez-Miller. Children's Press, 1986.

Other Books in the *Math By All Means* Series

*Burns, Marilyn. *Multiplication: Grade 3.* Math Solutions Publications, 1991.

*— . *Place Value, Grades 1–2.* Math Solutions Publications, 1994.

*— . *Probability, Grades 3–4.* Math Solutions Publications, 1995.

*Ohanian, Susan, and Marilyn Burns. *Division, Grades 3–4.* Math Solutions Publications, 1995.

*Rectanus,Cheryl. *Geometry, Grades 3–4.* Math Solutions Publications, 1994.

*These books are available from: Cuisenaire Co. of America, Inc.
P.O. Box 5026
White Plains, NY 10602-5026
(800) 237-3142

INDEX